Mrs A M Fraser
12 Southside Place
INVERNESS
IV2 3JF

D1625949

# THE
# INTERNATIONAL
## SCHOOL OF
# SUGARCRAFT
### BOOK TWO
ADVANCED

# THE INTERNATIONAL SCHOOL OF

# SUGARCRAFT

## BOOK TWO
### ADVANCED

*Principal Teacher*
## Nicholas Lodge

*Teachers*
## Ann Baber
## Lindsay Bradshaw
## Anne Smith
## Cynthia Venn

PREMIER
EDITIONS

Published in 1995 by Premier Editions
An imprint of Merehurst Limited
Ferry House, 51/57 Lacy Road,
London, SW15 1PR

ISBN 1 897730 60 8

A catalogue record for this book is available from the British Library.

Edited by Deborah Gray
Designed by Richard Slater
Photography by Graham Tann, assisted by Lucy Baker and Hilary Slater
Typeset by Angel Graphics
Colour separation by Fotographics Ltd, U.K. – Hong Kong
Printed in Italy by New Interlitho S.p.A., Milan

ACKNOWLEDGEMENTS
I would like to dedicate this book to Sindy for being there. My thanks to Robert
Venn, 3 Anker Lane, Stubbington, Fareham, Hants. PO14 3HF for the stand
featured on the cover of this book; to Alison Procter of Treelands, Hillside Road,
Bleadon, Weston-Super-Mare, Avon BS24 0AA for the posy pick with stand;
to Shirley Knight of Sugar & Ice of Litchfield House, 15 Cabstand, Portishead,
Bristol and B.R. Mathews & Son, 12 Gipsy Hill, Upper Norwood, London
SE19 1NN for items of equipment kindly given; to Monica and David and
Brenda Tyler.

The Publishers would like to thank the following for their help and advice:

B.R. Mathews & Son, 12 Gipsy Hill, Upper Norwood, London SE19 1NN
Ribbons from C.M. Offray & Son Limited, Firtree Place, Church Road,
Ashford, Middlesex CW15 2PH
Those products supplied by John F. Renshaw & Company Limited are readily
available from your local sugarcraft shop in the U.K., or by contacting John F.
Renshaw & Company Limited, Locks Lane, Mitcham, Surrey for overseas orders
Tate & Lyle Sugars, Enterprise House, 45 Homesdale Road, Bromley
Kent BR2 9TE

# Contents

## NICHOLAS LODGE

At the age of twenty-five, Nicholas has already achieved a great deal in his career with a fine list of credits behind him and experience working in several distinguished cake decorating companies and schools. Nicholas Lodge now lectures and demonstrates all over the world while continuing to run his own cake decorating and floristry business.

Nicholas has written the highly successful book 'Sugar Flowers' for Merehurst Press and more recently two books in 'The Art of Sugarcraft' series, 'Pastillage and Sugar Moulding' and 'Lace and Filigree'. As well as providing the framework for this book and overseeing its completion, Nicholas has contributed the beautiful chapters on the various aspects of flowerwork.

## ANN BABER

Ann Baber's versatile sugarcraft skills are renowned in the cake decorating world. Ann is an expert cake decorator, who is particularly skilled in working with chocolate and marzipan, as well as a capable businesswoman running her own cake decorating business in partnership with a former pupil.

Ann has contributed lessons on marzipan figure modelling, making chocolate eggs and figures and decorating with chocolate, all of which are important contributions to 'The International School of Sugarcraft'.

## LINDSAY JOHN BRADSHAW

Qualified as a chef, baker, confectioner and teacher, Lindsay John Bradshaw is one of Britain's top specialists in cake and confectionery design. He teaches at Salford College of Technology and also demonstrates cake decorating throughout the United Kingdom.

Merehurst has published the revised edition of Mr Bradshaw's 'Confectionery Design' which he previously published himself, he is also the author of 'Royal Iced Christmas Cakes'. Mr Bradshaw's lessons on filigree, advanced figure piping and freestanding runouts are valued contributions to this volume.

## ANNE SMITH

Anne Smith is still relatively new to the world of Sugarcraft. Her training is in the arts and her skills as a sculptor, potter and needlewoman provide a firm foundation for her excellent work in sugarpaste. Anne is currently Head of the Arts and Crafts Department at Bath Polytechnic and is eager to teach more sugarcraft classes and partake in more Sugarcraft competitions in the future.

Anne has also written the title on 'Sugarpaste' for the Merehurst series 'The Art of Sugarcraft' and has contributed the inspired lesson on Pastillage and Sugar Moulding to this book.

## CYNTHIA VENN

Cynthia Venn's cake decorating skills are well known and admired in the world of Sugarcraft. A teacher of Sugarcraft and an occasional contributor to magazines, she has established an interested following particularly in the application of needlework techniques to cake decorating. Cynthia is a frequent exhibitor and has won a number of national competitions.

Cynthia Venn taught cookery while establishing her own home catering business which she has now expanded to incorporate her enthusiasm for Sugarcraft. Cynthia has contributed the beautiful lessons on tube and brush embroidery, lace, extension work, bas relief, appliqué and smocking.

# FOREWORD

It is a pleasure and a privilege to write the foreword to this exciting book on advanced work in 'the wonderful world of Sugarcraft'. This book clearly illustrates a great many of the traditional techniques which have been taught to a high standard and used on classical and sugarpaste cakes as well as artistic pieces.

As a life-long enthusiast, teacher, and organizer of major London sugarcraft exhibitions and competitions, I know that this book will stimulate and encourage all those with a love of this age-old craft, and will build on the basic knowledge and skills learnt in Volume 1.

In any field of endeavour perfection can be accomplished by enthusiasm, imagination and practice and in this volume you will find a wealth of ideas upon which to develop your talents and establish an individual style.

I know that you will gain a life-time of happiness as you pursue the art of sugarcraft. I leave with you an appropriate quotation from the film world: 'to inspire awe and wonder; to create dreams.'

Eileen Swann
London 1988

# Decorating with Chocolate

# Decorating with Chocolate

As a decorative media, chocolate is not only attractive, but is a great favourite of young and old alike.

Chocolate marries well with most other flavours and colours, and may be used in combination with fresh cream, buttercream, crème pâtissière, marzipan and fondant. Decorating with chocolate can range from very simple grated shavings to more complicated piped trellis shapes. Melted chocolate can also be beaten into buttercream and crème pâtissière and used as a filling for gateaux, or stirred into fondant for coating or piping.

## INGREDIENTS
Chocolate buttons, chips or block chocolate may be used, preferably plain (semisweet or bitter) as this gives the best contrast to buttercream.
Chocolate-flavoured blocks can be used for much of this work.
Icing sugar
Liquid glucose

## EQUIPMENT
Double boiler or saucepan and china or glass basin
Wooden spoon
Palette knife
Greaseproof (waxed paper)
Cheese grater
Sharp pointed knife
Star piping tube
Pencil
Compass
Rolling pin
Paint scraper or butter pat roller
Cutters – round, fluted
Rose leaves

# Simple Chocolate Decorations

Take a cheese grater and using the large hole, grate a block of chocolate until you have enough for your requirement.

### Melting Chocolate
Melt some chocolate, either buttons or finely chopped block, in the following manner: put a saucepan of water on the stove to heat. Allow it to become very hot but not boiling. Place your chocolate chips either into the top of the double boiler or in a glass or china bowl. Remove the pan of hot water from the heat and stand the bowl of chocolate over the pan. Stir gently with a wooden spoon until the chocolate has completely melted.

### Piping Chocolate
Put some melted chocolate into a small cup and add some water, drop by drop, until your chocolate thickens to the consistency of buttercream. Stand the cup in hot water to keep the chocolate soft, because at this stage it will harden up very quickly. Put some of the piping chocolate into a greaseproof (waxed) paper piping bag. It will depend on what you are piping whether you have a tube or not. For much chocolate piping a tube is not necessary and simply seems to assist the hardening process more quickly. A star tube however is needed if a shell border is to be piped.

### Moulding Chocolate Roses
Roses and other simple flowers may be made as follows: mix equal quantities of melted chocolate with liquid glucose. Blend well together in a bowl with the aid of a wooden spoon. Turn out onto a clean work surface and knead briskly with the heel of the hand. It will feel a little like plasticine at this stage. Wrap in tin foil or cling film (plastic wrap) and use as soon as possible, to give a really high gloss to the rose petals.

### Making Cutout Shapes
Take an uncreased sheet of greaseproof (waxed) paper and pour some chocolate into the middle of it, making sure you have plenty of space all round. Quickly pick up each corner of the paper nearest you and lift it away from you. Then pick up the two edges of paper farthest away and roll the chocolate towards you. Repeat this process by turning the paper round and lifting the opposite sides. This spreads the chocolate out into a thin, even sheet, with no marks or indentations which you would get by using a palette knife. The last stage is to flap the paper up and down a few times to make sure there are no air bubbles. This thinly spread chocolate will soon dry and many interesting shapes can then be cut either with a knife, or with a shaped cutter.

**Chocolate Rolls or Cigars and Curls**
A marble slab is best for this process, however if unavailable, use a spotlessly clean plastic work surface instead. Pour some liquid chocolate onto the clean surface and very quickly spread it thinly backwards and forwards with a palette knife, increasing the area of the chocolate. Continue this until the chocolate starts to dry, and the palette knife leaves a mark. For rolls, take a 15cm (6in) blade fillet knife or any other thin-bladed sharp knife. Grasp the handle of the knife in your right

hand and place your left hand over it to add more pressure. Holding the blade nearly flat on top of the chocolate, draw it towards you. The chocolate will then curl into long thin cigar shapes. The longer the downward pull, the thicker the cigar.

Curls are made by preparing the chocolate in the same manner as for cigars , but the tool used is a 2.5-4cm (1-1½in) paint scraper. This time you push the scraper away from you, holding it in a more upright position than the knife. A butter curling tool

can also be used, but the curls will have a ridged effect.

**Curved Leaves**
These can be made by attaching greaseproof (waxed) paper to a rolling pin and with a little melted chocolate piping directly onto the curved surface. Piping chocolate must be used as ordinary melted chocolate would drop off the paper.

# Coloured Chocolate

**A**nyone who has been in Paris at Easter-time will have seen some of the wonderful displays of coloured chocolate birds and animals. The technique of colouring chocolate is simple, it may then be used decoratively in place of ordinary chocolate.

Colouring chocolate is not difficult, and the technique once mastered opens the gate to a whole new range of ideas.

### INGREDIENTS
White chocolate
Powdered food colouring
Liquid glucose
Glycerine-based food colouring

### EQUIPMENT
Saucepan
Glass or china bowl
Wooden spoon
Greaseproof (waxed) paper
Small palette knife
Small plastic cups
Small ladle or soup spoon
Cutter and moulds, if required

Heat a saucepan about one-third full of water until hot, but not boiling. Chop chocolate into small pieces and place in a bowl. Stand the bowl over the pan of water and gently stir with a wooden spoon until the chocolate has melted. The white chocolate will not be as runny as melted dark chocolate as it melts at a lower temperature, about 44°C (110°F).

White chocolate may be quite granular even when properly melted. Smooth chocolate may be obtained by standing a second bowl in hot water and pouring the chocolate into this through a very fine metal sieve. Take care to wipe the bottom of the first bowl after it has been lifted from the water as any drops of water falling into the melted chocolate will cause it to thicken and spoil. For this reason, do not use water-based liquid colouring.

Ladle a little chocolate into a plastic cup and add a little powdered colouring. Mix thoroughly until the chocolate is evenly blended. Place the coloured chocolate back into the bowl of melted chocolate and mix until the desired shade is reached.

**1.** Ladle the chocolate into a plastic cup.

**2.** Add the colouring a little at a time.

**3.** Stir to mix, adding more colour as required.

**4.** The white chocolate is now evenly coloured.

When making a variety of colours it is necessary to make each individually; however, colours can often be mixed to avoid the lengthy process of repetition. Moulding chocolate may be treated likewise.

Pale pink – can be turned into dark blue, purple, green and grey.

Lemon – can be turned into orange, peach, green and brown.

Always keep the chocolate standing in hot water to keep it liquid as white chocolate sets very quickly. If you are working with several colours simultaneously, stand the cups in a roasting tin half full of hot water.

## Cutouts

Ladle the chocolate onto a sheet of greaseproof (waxed) paper and spread quickly with a palette knife. You must work fast as white chocolate sets quickly. Pick up the edges of the paper and flap them up and down to remove air bubbles and knife marks. Leave until the chocolate is just set before cutting out shapes. For the best results work with small quantities of chocolate and repeat the process as necessary.

## Suggested Cutouts

Plaques: round or oval, fluted or plain.
Geometric shapes: squares, diamonds, circles and half moons.
Flowers: use blossom cutters in various sizes and leaves.
Figure cutters: use the cutter of your choice, such as Father Christmas, fir trees, rabbits, mice.

## Cutout variations

Chocolate cutouts may be piped with detail either by using royal icing or with coloured, milk or plain (sweet or semi-sweet) chocolate. One cutter may be superimposed upon another, for instance, a flower can be made with a dark centre attached to a paler outside; or a series of different coloured plaques may be combined. Cutouts may also be dusted with petal dust to achieve a shaded effect which is particularly attractive on flowers, leaves and butterflies. Leftover pieces of coloured chocolate may be broken into small pieces and finely chopped with a sharp knife. They may then be used like hundreds and thousands on the tops and sides of cakes. Store in an airtight container.

## Moulding Chocolate

Moulding chocolate is used to make flowers, leaves and small animals. Colour the chocolate before adding the glucose using either powder or paste colours. Equal quantities of liquid glucose and chocolate are then mixed together and kneaded as described above.

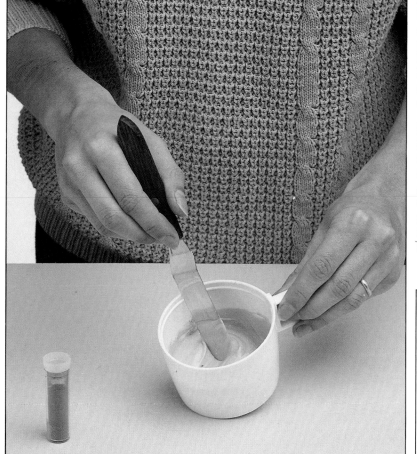

> ### EQUIPMENT
> Savoy bag
> Large star tube
> 30cm (12in) silver cake board
> Palette knife
> Turntable
> Cheese grater
> 7-10cm (3-4in) open circular cutter
> 2-4cm (1-1½in) circular cutter
> Greaseproof (waxed) paper
> Bowl
> Saucepan

# Gateau with Chocolate Disks

Sandwich sponges together with jam of choice and buttercream. Pipe in cream rather than spread it as this stops it sliding about on jam and gives depth to the sponge. Use a large star tube and savoy bag. Place sponge on a 30cm (12in) silver straw board.

Coat sponge all over with the buttercream, starting with the top until an even surface is achieved. Neaten edge with flat side of palette knife. Coat sides of gateau. This operation is much easier if you have a turntable. Divide sponge into equal portions.

Grate about 250g (8oz) of the chocolate and hold the sponge in one hand, with your hand flat on the bottom and pick up grated chocolate in the other hand. Bring together by tilting slightly and pressing chocolate onto sides of cake until evenly coated all round. Put back on cake board. Take the large circular cutter and place in the middle of gateau. Thickly sprinkle remaining grated chocolate covering the whole of the inside area of cutter. Gently remove cutter.

Cut some thin strips of paper 6m (¼in) and lay on top of the shavings. Dust thickly with icing (confectioner's) sugar. Carefully lift off paper. You will be left with an attractive striped effect.

Prepare some melted chocolate on a sheet of greaseproof (waxed) paper and with a small plain round cutter 2.5-3cm (1-1½in), cut out 12 circles of chocolate into each marked section of your gateau; pipe a whirl of buttercream on outside edge. Take a circle of chocolate and press lightly into buttercream whirl. Pick back off and turn over. Press plain side of circle back into whirl. The best results are achieved in a cool kitchen and the whirl and buttercream imprint are best made one at a time rather than all at once, as the first one will probably have dried too much to make a pattern on the chocolate.

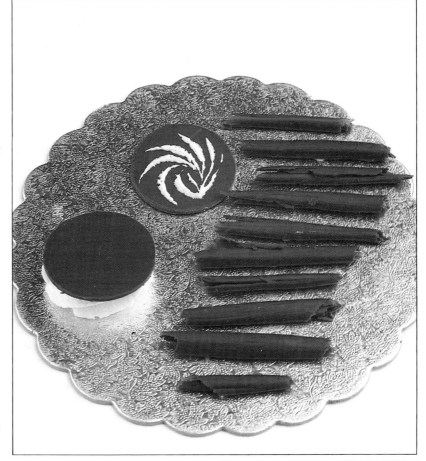

*Circles of chocolate for gateau with chocolate disk as seen on page 12, also showing chocolate cigars for rose gateau as seen on page 18.*

## INGREDIENTS
2x25cm (10in) whisked sponge cakes
500g (1lb/2½ cups) vanilla-flavoured buttercream
Strawberry or raspberry jam (jelly)
175g (12oz) plain (semisweet) chocolate
Icing (confectioner's) sugar

## VARIATIONS
Liqueur-flavoured Gateau: Whisked sponges absorb liqueur-flavoured syrups very well without disintegrating. Pour evenly over cake bases before coating.

## SYRUP
## INGREDIENTS
600ml (1 pint) water
500g (1lb) granulated sugar
Juice and zest of two lemons and one orange
12 coriander seeds
Cinnamon stick
Bay leaf

# Rose Gateau

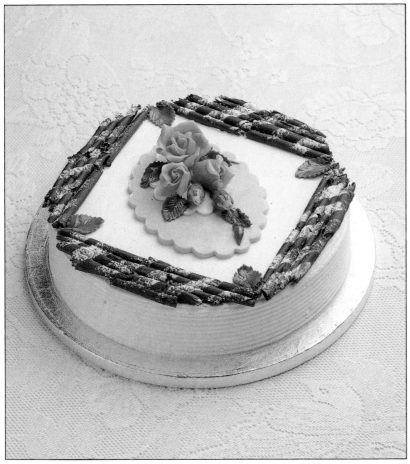

equidistant apart. Gently sieve the icing (confectioner's) sugar over the top, carefully remove paper strips. Place chocolate rose leaves in the corner of the rolls.

This gateau is not suitable for refrigeration, as if exposed to alternate cold and warm air, condensation will form on the chocolate causing the flowers to droop and become sticky; the icing (confectioner's) sugar would also dissolve.

## INGREDIENTS

2x25cm (10in) whisked sponge cakes
125g (4oz/1 cup) raspberry jam (jelly)
500g (1lb/2½ cups) vanilla-flavoured buttercream
250g (8oz) white chocolate
60g (2oz) liquid glucose
Pink powdered colouring
Christmas green paste colouring
250g (8oz) plain (semisweet) chocolate
Icing (confectioner's) sugar

## EQUIPMENT

28cm (11in) cake board
Turntable
Palette knife
Comb-edge scraper
Greaseproof (waxed) paper
14x12cm (5½x4in) oval cutter
8x5cm (3½x2in) oval cutter
Thin-bladed sharp knife
Scissors
Fine sieve or icing (confectioner's) sugar Dredger
Rose leaf cutter
2 saucepans
2 glass or china bowls
2 wooden spoons

## VARIATIONS

Pipe the recipient's name or the occasion, on the plaque or use sugar flowers. Tiny marzipan fruits could be arranged in a little mound while dark chocolate medallions attached to the white surface can look quite stunning.

## Method

Melt the white and plain (semisweet) chocolate in two separate bowls over pans of hot, not boiling water. Meanwhile, sandwich together the sponge cakes using about one-third of the buttercream. Use the remaining buttercream to cover the top and sides of the cake. Draw the comb scraper around the sides, neaten the edges, then smooth the top of the cake using a palette knife.

Ladle a little melted white chocolate onto some greaseproof (waxed) paper, flatten with a palette knife and flap the paper up and down to smooth and level. As soon as it is just set, cut out a small oval shape. Return remaining chocolate to the bowl. Following the procedure above, cut out a larger oval plaque in pink.

Colour the remaining pink chocolate to a darker shade of pink then add an equal quantity of liquid

glucose, mix with a wooden spoon, then turn out onto a clean surface and knead well. Cover with cling film (plastic wrap) and leave for about 15 minutes before making roses. When the roses are complete, colour the remaining moulding chocolate green for the leaves. Flatten a walnut-sized knob of chocolate between the thumb and forefinger, place on a flat surface and stamp out a rose leaf using the cutter. Mark veins on leaves with a sharp knife. Refrigerate leaves if they are too soft to handle.

Make about two dozen chocolate rolls from the plain (semisweet) chocolate. Fasten the small white plaque to the larger pink one and arrange the roses and leaves on top. Lift with palette knife onto the centre of the cake. Mark the cake into four and arrange chocolate rolls. Cut very thin strips of paper and arrange on the rolls

# Coffee Gateau

## INGREDIENTS

2x25cm (10in) coffee sponge bases
Apricot jam (jelly)
500g (1lb/2½ cups) coffee
buttercream
500g (1lb) dark (semisweet)
chocolate
1 walnut
12 angelica diamonds

## EQUIPMENT
Greaseproof (waxed) paper
30cm (12in) cake board
Pencil
Compass
Palette knife
Small sharp knife
Piping bag
Large star tube
Comb scraper
Turntable

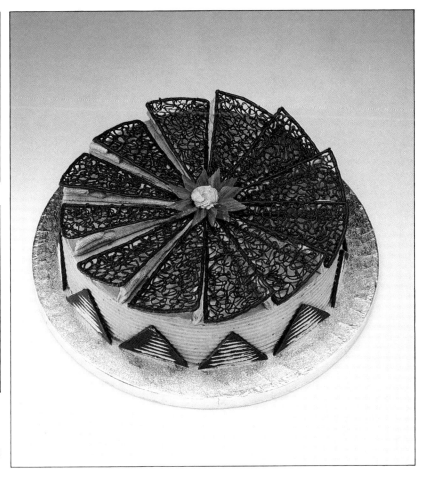

Spread apricot jam (jelly) on base of sponge. Pipe with coffee buttercream; smooth and flatten. Cover top of gateau fairly thickly with coffee buttercream. Smooth round with palette knife, then using a comb scraper, draw round sides of cake as if coating with royal icing. Place on cake board and mark top of cake into 12 equal sections.

Melt the chocolate. Draw a 25cm (10in) circle on a sheet of greaseproof (waxed) paper and, with the aid of a compass, divide it into 12 sections. On another sheet of greaseproof (waxed) paper pour some more chocolate and spread out thinly, allow to dry. Cut out six 3.5cm (1½in) squares of chocolate. Cut each one diagonally, giving 12 triangles. Stick these all round the base of the gateau by pressing slightly onto combed side, take back off, reverse and put plain side to edge of cake. The striped effect of coffee buttercream on dark chocolate is most attractive.

Take a little melted chocolate and pour into a small cup. Add a few drops of water until it has reached piping consistency. Put into a paper piping bag; cut off end of bag leaving a hole about the size of a No 2 plain piping tube. Pipe a fairly thick line round every other segment of your drawing. Repeat the process, but in every other segment, or do them one at a time. Put some more piping chocolate into another bag and pipe in between the chocolate frame in a squiggly pattern, making sure the chocolate touches the edges of frame and that the lines touch each other, (see detailed photograph). These pieces dry quite quickly. As they do so, ease off paper with a palette knife or by taking the paper to edge of table and gradually peeling off. As you complete each piece put to one side. On each segment of the gateau pipe a line of buttercream with 1cm (½in) plain tube from near centre to outside edge, pipe another on top 5cm (2in) along outside edge and a third on top of that about 2.5cm (1in) long. With the aid of a palette knife, lift up segments and prop each one against the line of cream until you have covered the top of the cake. Pipe a whirl of buttercream in the centre and decorate with a walnut and twelve angelica diamonds.

Small piped decoration that can be used on gateaux or fancies.

# Strawberry Chocolate Gateau

## Ingredients

25cm (10in) whisked sponge bases
Strawberry jam (jelly)
Small jar redcurrant jelly
250g (8oz) melted chocolate
125g (4oz) strawberries plus 12 even
sized strawberries
600ml (1pt/2½ cups) whipping
cream
60g (2oz/¼ cup) caster (superfine)
sugar
Icing (confectioner's) sugar
Kirsch

## Equipment

30cm (12in) cake board
Greaseproof (waxed) paper
Palette knife
Turntable
Whisk
Bowl
Saucepan
Icing (confectioners) sugar dredger
25cm (10in) cake tin (pan)
Sharp knife

### Method

Take two 25cm (10in) sponge bases and spread one with strawberry jam. Wash, hull and quarter about 125g (4oz) fresh strawberries. Place in a bowl and sprinkle with a little sugar and a few drops of kirsch if required. Whisk the cream to piping consistency and fold one-third of the cream into the strawberries. Spread onto jam and place the other sponge on top.

Spread remaining cream on top and side of gateau. Mark into 12 portions. Pour melted chocolate onto a sheet of greaseproof (waxed) paper. Proceed as for cutout shapes. Press grated chocolate round bottom edge of cake.

When set, place the 25cm (10in) sponge tin (pan) on the chocolate and cut round the tin using a sharp knife to produce a large chocolate circle. Using a long bladed knife cut circle into 12 even triangles. Melt some redcurrant jelly in a small saucepan adding just a little water to thin slightly. Wash and dry 12 even sized strawberries leaving on the green culots. Hold the culots and dip the strawberries into the jelly. Put onto greaseproof (waxed) paper to set. Place strawberries, thin edge to centre. Ease six chocolate segments off the paper and thickly dust with icing (confectioner's) sugar.

## Moulded Roses

To use this modelling paste and achieve the best results, allow to rest in a warm room for about an hour after making. When making the petals use only walnut-sized pieces at a time. Do not worry if it feels very greasy to the touch, this is because the warmth of the hand melts the cocoa butter in the chocolate. Mould a piece of the paste about the size of a little finger nail into a pear shape. Stand upright fat side down. Take a small piece of paste and roll between palms into a sausage shape. With thumb and forefinger of left hand, flatten out top piece of sausage. Hold the remainder with thumb and forefinger of right hand. Lay flattened edge in the palm of the hand with the tail pointing to outside edge of hand. With the thick end of a double ball tool, gently thin outside edge of petal. Hold petal with thumb and forefinger of left hand and with thumb and forefinger of right hand nip off surplus piece of sausage. The petals will be floppy, so lay flat on surface to set.

Make two petals about as big as thumb nail. Pick up centre-piece and lay on petal two-thirds to the left of it. Wrap left edge petal over centre. Take second petal and lay inside the first petal bringing round to overlap outside first petal. With thumb gently roll back outside edge of petals. The build up of the petals is as follows, tucking one inside the other until you have completed the sequence.

Bud – pear shape + 2 petals
Half rose – pear shape + 2 petals + 3 petals
Full rose – pear shape + 2 petals + 3 petals + 5 petals
Make each layer of petals slightly larger as they extend outwards.

*Suggested shapes for chocolate cutouts and piped decorations*

*Templates for designs illustrated in this lesson*

22

# Lesson 2

# Chocolate Eggs and Figures

# Chocolate Easter Eggs

**M**aking your own Easter eggs and chocolate moulded figures can be great fun. As well as gifts for the family, they can be given as presents to friends and children.

To be sure of success there are certain basic principles which have to be followed. Working with chocolate is not difficult providing you know the rules.

**Rule 1:** Buy the best quality moulding chocolate; chocolate-flavoured cake covering will not do.

**Rule 2:** Never overheat chocolate.

**Rule 3:** Never allow water or steam to get into the chocolate.

## INGREDIENTS
Chocolate buttons (chips) or block chocolate either milk (sweet), plain (semisweet) or white
Icing (confectioner's) sugar
Egg white
Food colouring for eggs, decorated with piped sugar flowers
Ribbons for eggs and rabbits.

## EQUIPMENT
Easter egg mould
Animal or figure moulds
Double saucepan or saucepan and china or glass basin
Wooden spoon
Small ladle
Greaseproof (waxed) paper
Piping tubes
Small sharp knife
Tissue paper

### Purchasing Materials
Most sugarcraft shops will stock all you need to make your eggs or moulded figures, and some hardware shops and supermarkets also sell moulds. Expensive plexi-glass moulds may also be hired or ordered specially. Many supermarkets as well as specialist shops now sell moulding chocolate, your local baker may also be able to sell it to you. Health stores will sell carob.

### Method
Check that your Easter egg mould is spotlessly clean and dry. The moulds are bought in halves and can be either smooth surfaced or a crazy paving pattern. When you are satisfied they are dry, take a clean, soft cloth and polish the inside. Put some water in the saucepan or bottom of the double boiler and place on the heat until very hot, but not boiling.

Half fill basin or top of double boiler with chocolate. If you have bought block chocolate cut it into small pieces before putting it into the basin. Stand basin of chocolate in the water. Stir gently with wooden spoon until chocolate has melted. It should be at a temperature of about 44°C

(110°F). Maximum workable temperature for plain (semisweet) chocolate is 49°C (120°F), it is not possible to work with chocolate that has been overheated. White and milk (sweet) chocolate should be used at a slightly lower temperature 42°C (105°F). If you do not have a thermometer, crook your little finger and touch the chocolate with the flat side. The chocolate should feel just warm (the correct heat).

Cut out some rectangles of greaseproof (waxed) paper slightly larger than the mould.

Pick up the Easter egg mould, holding the rounded part in the palm of your hand, and ladle in some chocolate until it is about one third full. Gently tilt the mould in all

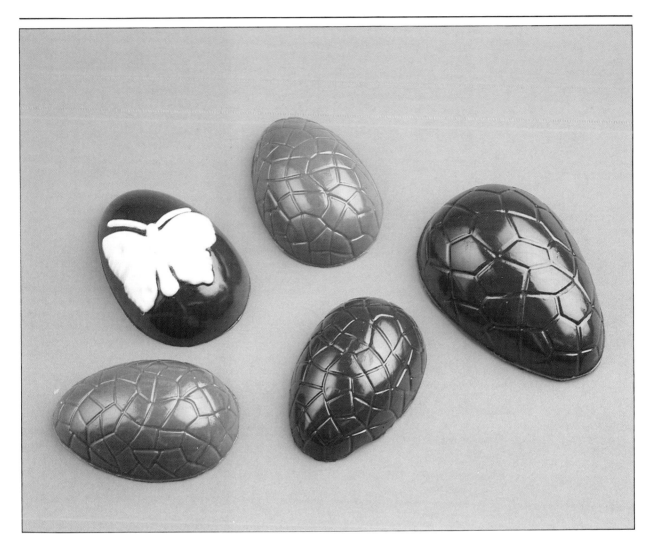

directions until the chocolate has covered the whole of the egg-shaped area. Hold the mould over the basin and turn it upside-down, allowing the surplus chocolate to drip out. Still upside-down, place the mould onto the cut rectangle of paper. Leave to dry. This takes about ten minutes.

If the water in the saucepan has cooled considerably, take out the basin of chocolate and pop the pan back on the stove and reheat water.

Check the inside of egg is dry by peeling off the paper. If dry, the chocolate should look dull. If you have a little ridge of chocolate inside the egg, shave it off with a sharp knife and put surplus back in basin. Refill the egg with liquid chocolate, repeating the same swilling and

emptying motion as before. Replace on greaseproof (waxed) paper.

Put the egg half or halves into the refrigerator. Look at the egg after 15 or 20 minutes. If the surface through the mould has taken on an overall silvery-grey colour, the egg is ready to be unmoulded. Remove from fridge and peel off the paper. Lay mould flat side down on paper. Hold each side of the flat edge of mould and gently pull sideways. The egg should then just drop out. Trim edges of the egg with a sharp knife.

To assemble, take a piece of tissue paper, fold it in half lengthwise, in half again and twist round into a rope shape, bring both ends together and tuck one around the other until you have formed a ring of tissue paper

with a hole in the middle. Chocolate should be handled as little as possible as it marks very easily. Lift the bottom half of the egg and place it hollow side up in your tissue paper nest.

If you wish to fill the egg with chocolates it is best to put some paper shavings into the bottom half of egg, as these will cushion the weight and stop the egg from breaking. So at this stage fill the lower half of egg with shavings, tucking them in neatly, and place in your chocolates.

Remove top half of egg from mould, using the same method as before. Gently holding egg, dip edges into melted chocolate and place over the bottom egg. This will seal the two halves together. Your egg is now ready to be decorated.

25

# Moulded Easter Eggs

**1.** Ladle melted chocolate into the egg mould until it is about one-third full.

**2.** Gently tilt the mould in all directions until the surface is completely covered.

**3.** Turn the mould upside-down and allow surplus chocolate to drip into the basin.

**4.** Place the mould on greaseproof (waxed) paper and refrigerate until set. Repeat steps 1–3.

**5.** The chocolate looks silvery when it is set, carefully unmould and trim the surplus chocolate from the edges of the mould using a sharp knife.

**6.** Diminishing sized eggs combined to create the Russian doll effect.

# Decorating Eggs

## Chocolate Decoration

Put a little melted chocolate in a small cup and add a few drops of water until it thickens to piping consistency. Put a small star tube into a piping bag. Scrape in chocolate and pipe shells round the join between the two halves. This looks very attractive if you have a milk chocolate egg and you pipe the shells in dark chocolate, and vice versa.

## Two Chocolate Egg

An attractive variation to single flavour Chocolate is to combine milk (sweet) with plain (semisweet) in the following manner: melt two basins of chocolate, one milk and one plain as in the method previously explained. Take some plain chocolate and put into a small cup. Thicken slightly with a few drops of water. Put into a piping bag without a tube. Cut off the end of bag, leaving a small hole. Pipe in a cornelli design all over the inside surface of the mould. Ladle in two coats of milk chocolate as previously described.

When stuck together pipe round the joins with dark chocolate. Decorate with chocolate roses and leaves.

## Royal Iced Decoration

Make up some royal icing. Tint to a colour of your choice. Put into a piping bag with a small star tube and pipe a shell border round the join between the two eggs.

The egg can be decorated with piped sugar flowers and leaves; bows; artificial flowers and fern; moulded chocolate roses and rose leaves; and particularly attractive is the piping of the recipient's name on the egg.

Clear cellophane boxes can be bought at most florists. The egg can be laid on coloured tissue paper and the box tied with a ribbon. Equally, proper Easter egg boxes are now available at most sugarcraft shops.

## Half Egg with Chicken

Take a half Easter egg and secure with melted chocolate upright on a cutout circle of chocolate about 6mm (¼in) thick. Pipe dot border of chocolate round circular base and attach a Garrett frill and bow around the outer edge of the egg. Fill base with miniature eggs and secure a small fluffy chicken sitting on top of eggs. Pipe the child's name on the flat base of chocolate, if desired.

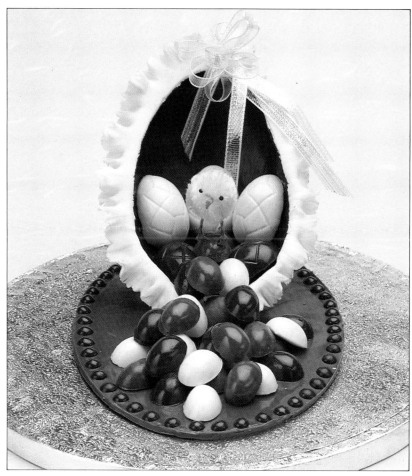

## Slimmer's Egg

Buy a balloon. Blow it up to about 10cm (4in) in diameter. Mark a line round half the balloon with pen. Lightly oil surface of balloon with vegetable oil and place thin end up, slightly angled, in a ring of tissue paper. Holding tied neck of balloon with one hand, pipe a border following the marked line.

Fill another piping bag with slightly stiffened chocolate. Do not use a tube, but cut off bag to make a hole approximately the size of a No2 plain piping tube. Pipe squiggles all over surface between shell piping, covering area well but leaving enough small spaces so that the finished effect is lacy. Allow to dry at room temperature. Pop the balloon, which will leave you with a lacy looking half Easter egg shape.

Secure the half onto an oval shaped base of chocolate. Place in base of egg, a single rose made from modelling chocolate, then arrange smaller roses, leaves and buds on the oval base.

# Chocolate Moulded Figures

As a change from Easter eggs small children love the Easter bunnies, ducks and other figures. In addition, many attractive moulds for Christmas figures to hang on the tree can now be purchased. Small moulded chocolate figures or space rockets can be an added extra to a child's birthday party as a take home gift. These smaller figures need about 30-60g (1-2oz) of chocolate and therefore are fairly inexpensive.

There are two main types of mould on the market: the half moulds where two sides are stuck together, as with the eggs, these are usually made in a soft, easy-care transparent plastic; or there are more expensive rigid plastic moulds, where the figure comes out all in one piece. These rigid moulds are in two halves which clip together and range from 5cm (2in) figures to ones several feet high.

---

| EQUIPMENT |
| :---: |
| Moulds |
| Double boiler or saucepan and basin |
| Glass or china bowl |
| Wooden spoon |
| Ladle |
| Greaseproof (waxed) paper |
| Small, sharp knife |
| Good quality block or button (chip) moulding chocolate |
| Ribbons |

## Chocolate Figures

The method of preparing the chocolate is fully explained in the Easter egg section. Exactly the same method should be followed for figure moulding, paying particular attention to the heating of the chocolate at all times.

The figure moulds are full of indentations, far more so than the Easter egg moulds, therefore special care must be taken to ensure each crevice is thoroughly clean and dry before use. Should the chocolate stick never try to gouge it out with a sharp knife or use a rough surfaced pad. Always wash mould in warm, soapy water, rinse with clean, warm water and dry thoroughly. Then polish mould with a soft, clean cloth.

Prepare chocolate. Cut squares or rectangles of greaseproof (waxed) paper larger than the base or flat side of mould. Half figures are made in exactly the same way as Easter eggs, swilling round the chocolate to cover all areas of the mould. However, because there are so many indentations it might be necessary to give the mould a sharp tap on the table to make sure all the cracks and crevices have been thoroughly coated. Reverse mould over basin and allow any surplus chocolate to drip back in. Place flat side down onto paper and allow to dry.

When dry, repeat the process with a second coating of chocolate; put back onto greaseproof (waxed) paper. Put into fridge until the silvery grey

appearance on the outside of the mould tells you that the chocolate is dry and has contracted away from the mould. Remove from fridge and turn out. Any surplus chocolate extending beyond the figure line can be carefully cut away with a small, sharp knife. The two halves of the figure can then be cemented together as previously mentioned for joining Easter eggs.

Bows can be tied round the necks of figures where appropriate, perhaps a different colour for each child, or with Christmas angels for example they can be tied with gold and silver thread and hung on the Christmas tree. Given as small gifts for unexpected visitors they should create an excellent impression.

## Rigid Plastic Figures

These moulds are quite costly but produce excellent results, making figures somewhat larger than the half moulds. The finished product requires less handling than the halves, and they are so well made that every detail of the figure stands out sharply. The moulds are tough and rigid and should last a lifetime. The average mould has between four and five strong metal clips to hold the two sides together. An 18cm (7in) high bunny takes about 75g (2½oz) of chocolate.

### Method

Check that the mould is spotlessly clean and dry, paying particular attention to the ears, nose and tail or similar indentations with other moulds. Polish well. Clip together. Prepare chocolate. Cut out square of greaseproof (waxed) paper larger than base of figure.

Hold mould upside down, and ladle in chocolate, half filling mould. Tap sharply to get rid of any air bubbles which might be trapped. With a tilting action towards you, gently roll the mould round and round. Bring the

chocolate evenly towards the base of the mould. It is best to do this holding it over the basin, so that surplus chocolate will drip straight into the basin. When the chocolate has stopped dripping, look down through the mould, holding it to the light. If you can see daylight anywhere this means the chocolate was slightly too warm and slid off the surface. Recoat with more chocolate.

Stand mould upright on paper and leave until dry. Recoat the inside of mould. There is no need to tap this time, but roll chocolate down to the base in the same manner as before. Drain over basin. When the chocolate has stopped dripping, place on a square of greaseproof (waxed) paper and put into fridge. Leave in fridge for 20 to 30 minutes until the mould has taken on a silvery-grey appearance. Remove from fridge.

Take off clips. Slide the point of a sharp knife or thumb nail between the join of the two halves of mould. One half of the mould should just come away. Lay the figure, exposed chocolate side down, hold each side of the mould with fingers pulling sideways, and at the same time press down on mould with thumbs. This should release the figure. Handle as little as possible. Stand upright, and place on bow around the neck where suitable.

## Making Rigid Plastic Figures

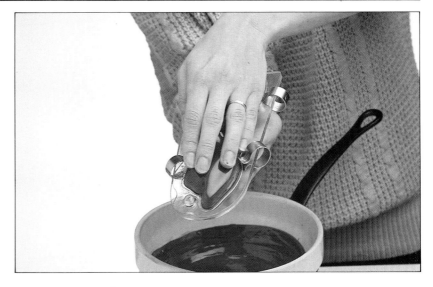

**1.** Ladle the chocolate into the mould, roll round until the entire figure is thoroughly coated with chocolate.

**2.** Drain the excess chocolate from the mould into the basin.

**3.** Stand on paper and chill until set and silvery-grey.

**4.** To unmould, remove the clips from the side of the mould by pressing firmly with the thumbs.

**5.** Pull the mould apart gently

## Decorative Ideas

With rabbits particularly or with the angels, melt a little white chocolate and pipe into ear and tail, or wing cavities. Then proceed with a double coating of chocolate.

Milk and plain (sweet and semisweet) chocolate can be used together to highlight any feature in the mould of your choice. Rabbits of varying sizes can be made and placed on a cake top covered in green marzipan that has been pushed through a sieve to resemble grass.

# Marzipan Figure Modelling

# Marzipan Figures

**M**aking your own marzipan figures is great fun and with a little practice excellent results can be achieved.

Marzipan is made from ground almonds and caster (superfine) sugar plus egg white and sometimes liquid glucose. Because of the high percentage of oil in the almonds, working with the paste under certain conditions means it becomes rather oily. It is best not to make figures in damp humid weather if it can be avoided. The paste becomes very soft and sticky, difficult to handle and the figures will droop. However, a little dry icing (confectioner's) sugar worked into the paste will help to stiffen it up.

For figure modelling the white marzipan is most appropriate because it is easy to colour, and some animals, such as the panda, require white marzipan. Good quality white marzipan is on sale in most supermarkets these days. Sugarcraft shops always have a plentiful supply. If making your own, it is best to use icing sugar with the ground almonds as this will produce a smoother textured paste with which to work.

Always work with clean utensils, hands and work surfaces and wash hands frequently as they will become sticky. Always dry hands thoroughly as damp hands will make the paste tacky. Use icing sugar to keep hands and table surface dry. Never use flour as this will cause fermentation, cornflour causes cracking and leaves white patches in coloured paste and caster sugar is too granular.

Paste can be coloured with either dust or paste colours. It is not wise to use liquid food colourings as they make the marzipan sticky, particularly if a strong or dark colour is required.

The marzipan figures will dry off very well at normal room temperature, but keep away from strong sunlight which will soften the paste causing the figures to wilt. Never put completed figures into plastic boxes, covered tins or shut away in kitchen cupboards as this will also cause the marzipan to soften and the figures to disintegrate. It takes a very long time for the figure to go rock hard, at least six months, after which

time it does not taste very good.

There are many recipes for making your own marzipan, a selection of which have been given in book 1. However, the rule of thumb is twice the amount of icing sugar to ground almonds and 60g (2oz) egg white to 500g (1lb) dry ingredients. For the real perfectionist, a professional recipe used by the experts is:
400g (14oz) raw marzipan
50g (2½oz) liquid glucose
300g (10oz/2½ cups) icing (confectioner's) sugar

Marzipan should be stored in a sealed plastic bag to keep it pliable and to stop a crust from forming. If you do have a crust, cut it off with a sharp knife and check that no fermentation has taken place by smelling it. Re-knead before use.

Never try to knead in bits of hard crust, as they will not soften and simply make figure moulding impossible.

## EQUIPMENT
Food colouring, powder or paste
Royal icing for piping eyes and small details
Cocktail sticks
Small rolling pin
Small scissors
Egg white
Marzipan modelling tools
Stamens with the ends cut off for whiskers

# Prehistoric Range

These are a great favourite with small children, who simply love eating the monsters.

Each of the figures weighs approximately 60g (2oz). Over that weight and they tend to become ungainly. Average height is 5cm (2in) and overall length 7.5cm (3in). Some figures are fashioned from one piece of marzipan, others comprise of as many as ten separate pieces.

| INGREDIENTS |
| --- |
| 60g (2oz) marzipan per figure |
| Royal icing |
| Egg white |
| Dust or paste food colouring |
| Dry icing (confectioner's) sugar |

| EQUIPMENT |
| --- |
| Piping bags |
| Scissors |
| Small sharp knife |
| Cocktail sticks |
| Paintbrush. |

## Brontosaurus

Colour 60g (2oz) marzipan a dark, coffee brown colour. Roll between palms of hands to a pear shape. Press lightly on work surface, dusted with icing (confectioner's) sugar to flatten bottom. Pull out tail from sharp end of pear shape. Flatten and round off.

Holding the body in one hand, start to pull out neck from far end of body. When it is about 5cm (2in) long, bend over 2cm (¾in) to form the head.

Push a cocktail stick down the length of the neck to support it. With the back of a small knife, cut a slit in the lower part of the head for the mouth. Pinch out feet from the main body, the front ones being well forward. Flatten and mark claws with the back of knife. Mark the body all over with the tip of a sharp knife to give the skin a textured look. Pipe in eyes, use a large dot of white and a smaller dot of chocolate. The placing of the chocolate dot will determine the expression on the face.

NOTE: Any small child eating this animal must be warned of the cocktail stick in the neck.

# Tyrannosaurus

Colour 60g (2oz) marzipan green. Divide into two. Roll one piece into an elongated pear shape. Bend the thinner end to lift up, while holding fatter end pressed down on work surface until the piece will stand upright by itself with the tail flicking up slightly. With the scissors make two cuts near top of fattest part, keeping tail to the back. Flatten the cut pieces with thumb and forefinger to form the paws. Divide the remaining paste in half. Take one piece and roll into a ball. Gradually square off ball stroking one side downwards for front of head. This will also elongate it slightly at the same time. Cut slit in head for mouth and attach to body with egg white. Cut two thin strips out of the almond for teeth and stick each side of mouth. Divide the remaining paste in two and roll into sausages about 2.5cm (1in) long. Form into reverse S shape and flatten one end to represent paws. Stick legs either side of body with egg white. Take a No3 plain piping tube and gently poke all over body. Pipe in eyes.

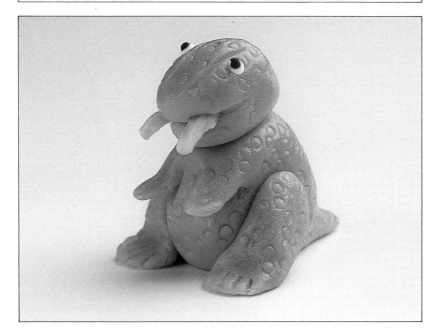

# Stegosaurus

Colour a piece of marzipan the size of a thumb nail a light, coffee colour. Roll out with a rolling pin until about 5.5cm (2½in) long and 12mm (½in) wide. With a round fluted cutter, cut frill. With a sharp knife trim off in a curve following line of scallops making it thinner at each end. With remaining spare piece cut out the horn for the tail.

Between palms of hands roll marzipan into a ball, and with outside edges of hand gently roll each end of ball to give it a double ended pear shape. Pull out and flatten one end for the tail. Pull out other end but keep more rounded for the head. Cut slit for mouth with the back of a knife.

Pull out feet by pinching marzipan between finger and thumb. Mark claws. Paint a little egg white down the spine of the animal and attach the scalloped piece. Attach the horn with a dot of egg white. Pipe eyes as for brontosaurus.

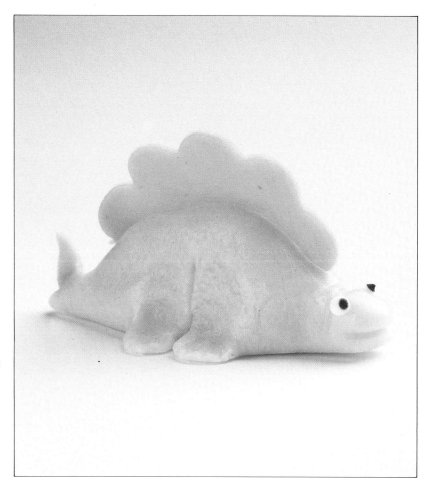

# Dimetrodon

Colour 60g (2oz) marzipan with edible plum dusting powder. Break off about one-eighth of the paste. Roll this out thinly and cut out a half moon shape about 5.5cm (2½in). Mark with back of knife. Divide remainder into four balls. Elongate slightly, flatten one end and mark in claws.

With rest of the paste roll into a flat cigar shape. Pull out tail. The head is rather like that of a tortoise, so when pulling keep it rounded rather than flat or pointed. With the back of a knife gently press the area between head and body to give a distinct division. Mark body all over by gently pressing sharp side of knife to make very shallow cuts. Cut slit for mouth. Attach feet and thin frill on back with egg white. Pipe in eyes as for brontosaurus.

# Wild Animals

## Baby Seal

Divide white paste into four. Take two small finger nail sized pieces of white paste. Roll into sausages 18mm (¾in) long and flatten out to 12mm (½in) wide for flippers. Mark paws with a sharp knife.

Roll three-quarters of the marzipan into a long pear. Taper end then flatten out. Snip end and flatten each half with thumb and forefinger to represent tail. Fasten flippers with egg white each side of front of body. Roll the remaining marzipan into a ball, pinch out centre to a point. With forefinger flatten the point and push back into the head to make the little rounded nose. Stick on head with nose in line with front right flipper. Put some chocolate icing in a bag with a No0 tube. Pipe tiny dots all over seal.

Pipe in nose and mouth. To give the seal an endearing look, pipe large eyes in chocolate only. Affix three black stamens each side of the nose to represent whiskers.

# Whale

Colour tiny piece of paste pink. Make two balls, flattened out about 6mm (¼in) across. Colour three-quarters of remaining paste black. Pinch off enough to make three fins. Two side fins are small sausages 2.5cm (1in) long flattened to 6mm (¼in) wide. Back fin is shaped slightly thicker at base and fractionally curved with a rounded tip. Start with 12mm (½in) long sausage shape. The main body of black is moulded like a cigar, the tail pulled out and then flattened. Make a central snip with scissors then flatten. Bend upwards. Flatten underside of body by pressing onto work surface. With forefinger, flatten front end of nose and bend upwards slightly.

Roll white paste like a cigar. Taper one end and flatten for mouth. Flatten part that is to be fitted onto the black upper part of body. Pinch up two pieces either side and pull slightly forward. Fasten two pieces of body with egg white, pressing and moulding together, keeping mouth well open. Stick in pink tongue. Secure side fins pointing slightly backward, then top fin in lower middle of back. Pipe in eyes. If the tail will not stay curved up, support for several hours to secure.

# Raccoon

Colour 60g (2oz) marzipan light brown. Pinch off a little ball about the size of a small finger nail and colour it dark brown. These are for the two stripes round the tail, paws on feet and patches on face. Roll out very thinly, cut two strips 6mm x 2.5cm (¼ x 1in) for tail; two pear drops for the face (can be done with aspic cutter), and 6mm (¼in) circle for feet. Cut circle in half and flatten out slightly.

Take two-thirds of the remaining paste and roll into ball for the body, press onto surface lightly until it will stand on its own. With a sharp knife make two downward cuts 12mm (½in) in from each side of ball halfway down the body. Pull out to form legs, press ends flat to represent paws. With remaining one-third of paste, nip off about one-quarter and divide in half. With one half roll into a sausage, making it thinner at one end for the tail. To assemble, fasten dark brown stripes of marzipan round tail. Tuck under back of body securing with egg white. Attach head, arms and brown pieces on paws with egg white. With the other half roll into a sausage about 5cm (2in) long. Cut in half. Flatten one end of each small piece for paws. With remaining paste, roll into a ball and with thumb and forefinger gently pull out into a pointed shape from centre of ball to represent nose. Pinch out ears and hollow slightly with ball tool. Put some white icing into a bag and pipe on a face. Smooth over with a very slightly damp paintbrush. Attach pear drop shapes onto wet icing. Ease into position with a cocktail stick. Pipe a little white icing in ear cavity, tips of arm, paws and eyes. Finish by piping brown nose, claws and eye centres.

## Squirrel

Colour 60g (2oz) marzipan a reddish brown colour. Divide in half. Roll one half into a pear shape, press onto surface flat side down and lean slightly forward. Divide rest of paste into three pieces. Roll one-third into a sausage 5cm (2in) long for the tail making it fatter at one end. With a small, sharp pair of scissors make little cuts pointing upwards all over the tail. With another third, fashion face, making it rather pointed, and flatten either side of point to represent the fat cheeks. Pinch up ears and hollow with small ball tool. With remaining marzipan, take about a quarter to make two little sausages for arms and two larger sausages for legs. Bend the larger sausages into a reverse S shape for legs. Flatten one end of each for paws. To assemble, tuck tail under body and prop up with foam until set. Fasten all remaining pieces in position with egg white. Pipe in eyes and a little cross in chocolate icing to represent nose.

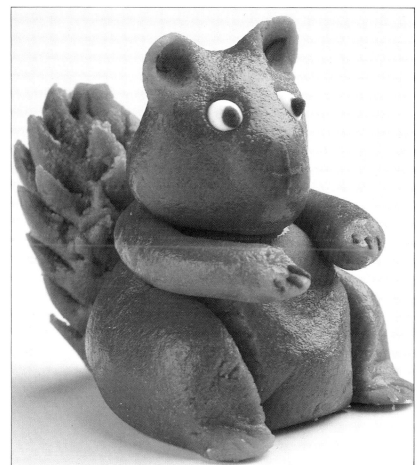

## Panda

Colour one-third of the marzipan black. For the arms take half of the black paste and roll into a sausage about 6cm (2½in) long. Bend round into a half moon. Pinch off two small pieces of black paste about the size of a little finger nail. Form into balls and flatten out for ears. With a ball tool, hollow out the centre. Take another tiny piece of black, flatten out and cut two tiny pear drops for facial markings. Reserve a minute piece of the remaining black for the nose then divide the rest in half. Roll into fat sausages 18mm (¾in) long. Curve inwards slightly, pinch up ends and flatten for feet. Divide the white paste into two, one slightly larger than the other. Take a tiny piece off the smaller ball, roll into a ball, stick black nose on.

Roll white body into a ball. Press base flat. Roll head into a round shape. Stick on nose. Make two indentations with back of knife under black piece pointing downwards at an angle. Either side of nose fasten pear drops, thicker end uppermost. Stick on ears. Fasten arms with egg white onto top of body and attach legs either side, with the inside curve of the legs tucking round body. Stick head into position securely.

# Woodland Scene

Put 60g (2oz) vanilla buttercream to one side, colour the remainder brown using chocolate or food-colouring. Coat board with one-third of brown buttercream. Unroll the white swiss (jelly) roll and wrap it round the chocolate one. Stand upright on board towards back. Cut the other swiss roll at an angle and stick with buttercream, pointed side down to side of main roll. Unwrap any remaining swiss roll and wrap round base of upright log, to give a

thick looking base. Spread brown buttercream thickly all over log and branch, leaving a flat surface. Fork upwards to make the surface look like bark. Spread the 60g (2oz) vanilla buttercream onto the flat surface of log. Pipe tree rings in chocolate icing.

Take 500g (1lb) marzipan and colour it green. Press small pieces at a time through a wire mesh sieve to resemble grass. Slice off with sharp knife and place all over board and round tree

trunk. Use the remaining marzipan to make the animals
125g (4oz) light brown for raccoon x 2
125g (4oz) red for toadstools x 4
125g (4oz) red brown for squirrel x 2
15g (½oz) grey for mouse
15g (½oz) pink for flowers
250g (8oz) dark brown for small log and rabbits
some white dots for toadstools.

## Small Log

Take 60g (2oz) marzipan coloured dark brown. Roll into a sausage shape about 10cm (4in) long. Hollow out ends with the tip of a sharp knife. Score with the knife all over log to look like bark.

## Toadstools

For the stalk, make a fat sausage shape thicker at one end. Stand firmly on surface to flatten end. The cap is made from a ball of paste flattened on one side with the edges pulled thinner with finger and thumb. Attach the two pieces with egg white. The white paste for the spots is rolled out and cut out

with the knob end of a pen, attach with egg white.

## Ivy

Pipe ivy stems at random round the log, then stamp out leaves from some green sugarpaste with a small ivy leaf cutter. Attach to the stems around cake.

## Flowers

Roll out pink paste thinly and cut out with tiny blossom spring cutter. Arrange in clumps on grass in between the animals.

### INGREDIENTS

500g (1lb) vanilla buttercream
3 swiss (jelly) rolls,
chocolate and white
1.2kg (2½lb) marzipan
Royal icing
125g (4oz) green sugarpaste

### EQUIPMENT

Piping bags
Small ivy leaf cutter
30cm (12in) cake board
Sharp knife
Scissors
Tiny blossom cutter with spring

# Human Figures

**F**igure modelling is an enjoyable, but time consuming activity. Although appreciated by children as decorations for cakes, these figures would also make excellent showpieces for exhibitions and competitions.

These nursery characters represent two methods of figure modelling. Marzipan is a heavy material to work with and, ideally, the figures should be kept small to prevent the marzipan bending and breaking. The girl figure is 15cm (6in) high and is supported by a wooden dowel which is hidden beneath her skirt. Figures with two legs are much more unstable and should generally be smaller, the gnomes are about 8cm (3½in) and are supported by a cocktail stick, inserted through the body and part of the head. Do not forget to warn children that these figures contain supports and should not be eaten.

## Gnomes

### Head
Colour 15g (½oz) marzipan to a flesh tone. Roll into a ball and elongate slightly to form jowls, indent eyes with a ball tool. Take two tiny balls of flesh-coloured paste and flatten into a triangle for the hands, mark in fingers with a sharp knife. Colour a minute piece dark pink for the nose.

Colour 8g (¼oz) marzipan brown, mould into two pear shapes and, with a ball tool, hollow out the fat end to stand the legs into. Ease up sides slightly. Colour a small ball of marzipan black for the belt, roll into a long sausage. Divide the remaining paste into three and colour brightly for the trousers, jacket and cap.

### Trousers
Roll into a rectangular ball and make a cut in the middle of one short side, ease two pieces apart and round off for the legs. Flatten the base of each leg and stand into the shoes securing with a little egg white.

### Jacket
Roll into a rectangular ball and with finger and thumb hollow into a bell shape, cut a small V in the centre. Fasten with egg white onto the trousers. Push a cocktail stick through the body leaving 12mm (½in) protruding to attach the head. Roll out two small sausages for the arms and mould into

shape. Attach to the body at the shoulder and stick on the hands.

### Finishing
Make an elongated pear shape and hollow out until it is large enough to fit onto the head. Leave pointing upwards or bend as desired. Stick the cap onto the head and attach the head to the body. Stick the nose in place. Make a small triangle and elongate for the beard. Pipe white icing for the eyes and brush white icing onto the beard. Paint in features when the icing has dried. Stick belt around the waist and pipe in the buckle.

## Girl

### Head and Body
Dust the plaster head moulds with a little cornflour (cornstarch) and press flesh-coloured marzipan into each half, trim any surplus marzipan level with the mould. Unmould and stick the two halves together with a little egg white, smooth the join with thumbs. With about seven-eighths of the remaining flesh-coloured marzipan, mould into a body shape emphasizing the waist. Insert dowel through the centre of the moulded piece.

### Skirt
Roll the blue marzipan thinly and cut out a circle, the radius should equal the body length from the waist to the base. Cut a hole in the centre of the skirt and position securing around the waist with egg white. Arrange the flounces.

---

### INGREDIENTS

125g (4oz) marzipan
Food colouring
Royal icing
Cocktail stick

---

### Arms
Fold the wire pieces in half and twist all strands together. Cut off two lengths for the arms in proportion to the body. Make two sausages from the remaining flesh-coloured marzipan and mould around the wire leaving about 6mm (¼in) exposed at one end, bend into shape. Flatten the other end for the hands and score the fingers with a knife. For the sleeves, roll two pieces of red marzipan into fingernail-size balls. Flatten slightly, make four indentations in the rounded edges and attach to the surplus wire on the arms. Pipe white royal icing into the indentations.

### Hair
Divide the black marzipan in half. Roll one half into a ball, hollow out with the thumbs to form a cap large enough to fit over the head for the hair. Elongate the back of the hair and stick into position. Mark a parting with a knife. Roll out a tiny piece of red for the ribbon and bow and attach.

### Bodice
Roll out a rectangle with the remaining black paste, the width should be half the circumference of the bust and the length should be twice the length from the neck to the waist. Cut a hole for the neck section and fashion the front into a V shape. Ease over the body and smooth the side joins. Attach sleeves, arms and head. Paint in face.

### INGREDIENTS
165g (5½oz) marzipan
Royal icing
Egg white
Food colouring

Colour marzipan as follows:
90g (3oz) marzipan flesh colour
45g (1½oz) blue
15g (½oz) black
15g (½oz) red

### EQUIPMENT

13cm (5in) piece of dowel
Plaster face mould
2 pieces of 24-gauge covered wire
No 00 paintbrush
Small rolling pin
Sharp knife

# Pastillage and Sugar Miniatures

# Figure Modelling

**P**re-formed moulds are readily available and will produce competent figures but the poses and sizes available are restricted. Far more original and lifelike results can be attained by building up the figure freely with the use of an armature (wire support).

If the figure or animal is to be dressed, the body itself can be a fairly rough shape as it will be hidden and the areas that will be visible such as the arms and head can be modelled in greater detail. One important point to remember is that the addition of clothes will enlarge the figure so that the body needs to be thinner and needs to be thoroughly dry before clothing is added otherwise cracking will occur.

Proportions are very important when modelling human figures. The head should measure one-sixth of the body size. When modelling a child, this proportion is different. The head is much larger and will roughly measure a quarter of the body size. When the arms are held at the side of the body, the fingers should reach mid-thigh. Many people tend to make the arms far too short and this will spoil the balance of the figure. Ask someone to pose if possible so that a natural position can be achieved.

## The Face

This is the most important area as it tends to be the focal point of the figure and the whole effect can be spoiled if, for instance, a flower fairy, Goldilocks or baby has a cracked or lined face with a crooked nose. A mould can be made from plaster using a doll's head cut in half. The head then can be formed by pushing a small ball of paste into the mould so that the features are formed on one side and the back part of the ball forms the back of the head.

When painting on the features, the eyes should focus on an area within the modelled scene, so that they don't appear vacant or staring. Paint the iris (the coloured area of the eye). When dry, paint the black pupil and again, when dry, highlight with a dot of white. This should bring some life to the eyes. Blush the cheeks with dusting powder, lightly add freckles, if desired, with minute dots of paprika paste colour. Paint lips also with paprika, not bright red or bright pink.

Hair can be piped with royal icing or it can be made by pushing soft paste through a garlic press or a potter's clay gun. It could also be rolled with the fingers into fine strands. It can be applied to form tight curls or, by using the gun, plaits or ringlets.

## Modelling Animals

When modelling animals, try to work from photographs, real life or illustrations so that the pose is correct and most important, the colour and markings of the fur and formation of paws and features are correct and a realistic likeness is achieved. The body shape and pose are important if it is to bear any resemblance to that particular creature even if an animal is to be dressed or is a fantasy animal.

## Cards, Caskets and Moulded Decorations

Again, moulds can be used to produce bells, caskets, slippers and any other basic shape, but it is far more rewarding to produce something that is truly original. Look for more unusual moulds, for example a flower pot, doll's shoes, aspic dishes. Templates can be cut and made for cards, caskets and houses for a more personal result.

## Paste

For the rough body shapes or anything that will be hidden with royal icing or clothes, use gelatine paste. For finer detailed work, clothes, faces, hands, for instance, use fine flower paste or modelling paste.

## Breakages

It is advisable to make spares if any item is particularly fragile, for example cards and caskets, in case of breakages because of time involved in the drying process.

## Use of Wire and Plaster Moulds

A warning must be given if wire, plaster moulds or cocktail sticks have been used to support the modelling in case it is eaten by a child.

# Pastillage Cards

**Pastillage Cards**

It is important to dry the pieces on a completely flat surface, lightly dusted with cornflour (cornstarch). Roll some paste out thinly. Cut the card shape on the surface on which it is to be dried. Do not attempt to lift and transfer the piece after any cutout shapes have been removed, as this could distort the overall shape. Cut the card shape with a very sharp knife. Use a single rocking movement, do not drag the knife as this will stretch and distort the paste. Cut in from the corners, not out to the corners. When drying turn the pieces so that they will dry flat and will not warp.

**Heart-shaped Card**

Cut out card pieces as above. Use a biscuit cutter to remove the heart shape from the front card. Cut a heart shape in paste, medium thickness, place on inside face. Smooth the edge with fingers and modelling tool to give a padded effect. Paint a monogram on the inside of the raised heart. Pipe an edge with royal icing around the padded heart on the inside and also round the cutout heart edge.

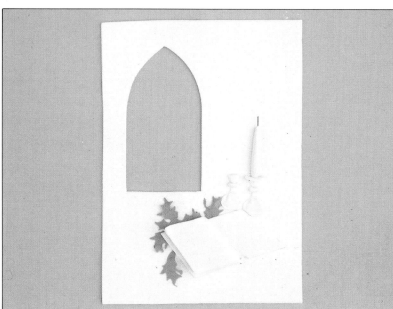

## Confirmation Card

Cut out window on front face. Form base of candlestick by cutting out shape quite thickly and indenting with a modelling tool and rounding edges to give a three dimensional look. Build up the top of the candlestick and make an indentation large enough for the candle to be placed inside. Make two thin sausage shapes, tapering at one end for the candle, insert black stamen cotton for wick. Support with foam until set so that the candle will stand away from the card.

Cut out chrysanthemum leaves. Place around edge of book area. Cut out the cover of the book and indent the spine. Place on a thick rectangle of sugarpaste for pages of book. Round the edges at the centre of the book. Cut out a single page from a thin piece of paste. Turn up edges and support with the fine slivers of foam until dry. Add writing with No00 brush. Dust the surface of the pages with cream powder and gold sparkle. Add chrysanthemums. Position a thin piece of paste for the ribbon bookmark.

On the inside face, paint the church window using paste colours. Use clear, pastel colours. Write the verse with a fine, non-toxic pen.

## To Assemble Cards

Pipe a snailstrail along inside edge of inner card. Place the two cards together. Support until dry. Pipe another decorative edging on spine of the card to strengthen.

# Bramble Mice

**Mother Mouse**

Make a rough shape for the body using gelatine paste. Allow to dry thoroughly. Colour flower paste blue. Roll out paste quite finely. Using the pattern, cut out the bodice and attach to body. Cut out the skirt. Fold and drape pleats, mostly at the back of the skirt and place around the body. Place the seams at the front of the figure so that they will be hidden by the apron. Make a bustle from a thick piece of paste. Place at the back of the figure and attach to the skirt.

**Head**

Make a small cone, indent eyes, nostrils and mouth, paint in facial markings. Make mop cap by rolling a small ball of paste, indent with large ball tool, pinch edge around indentation and place on the mouse's

head. Make ears with pinky grey paste, first make a small ball, flatten and indent with a ball tool. Pinch together the base of the ear and attach to the hat. Use a cocktail stick and frill a long narrow piece of paste and attach to the edge of the cap. Roll two small balls of black paste and place into eye sockets. Texture the surface of the paste with a scalpel to look like fur. Cut out apron skirt and frill edge, apply to dress. Cut out apron bib, attach to body (try to hide the waist seam). Make two ribbon ties and a bow, attach to back of apron. Paint a pattern on the dress with a fine paintbrush.

**Arms**

Make a long sausage shape in pinky grey colour paste. Flatten one end to form a spade shape. Cut four long,

thin fingers. Pinch and round ends of fingers. Place paw on foam and indent with a ball tool to curl fingers. Thin out the wrist, shape arm. Place in a curved position and leave to dry. When dry, wrap the sleeve paste around the arm. Attach to the body with royal icing, support until dry.

**The Egg Cradle**

Roll out a piece of paste of medium thickness, dust a small egg with cornflour (cornstarch). Drape the paste over the egg. Smooth the paste carefully downwards so that the paste follows the shape of the egg. Cut the jagged points with a scalpel, remove paste from the egg and lightly smooth edges. Replace paste onto the egg until dry. When dry, place a sugarpaste mattress inside the egg so that the baby mouse will be upwards when placed inside and become more visible. Make a pillow out of a roughly square piece of sugarpaste. Pinch the corners to give a natural look. Frill a thin, narrow piece of flower-paste to form lace edging. Make a small head as for mother mouse. Make a rough conical shape for the body from sugarpaste. Roll out a thin piece of paste for blanket. Fold and tuck in the edges. When dry, dust yellow and paint on a flowered pattern with a fine brush. Dust egg blue, add on brown markings with a fairly dry paintbrush using brown paste colour.

Prepare plaque by colouring gelatine crystals with green dusting colour. Cover area with gum arabic or egg white, sprinkle on crystals. Tip away excess. Make blackberry leaves, (see page 219), arrange in a spray. Attach to the plaque with royal icing along with the egg and mother mouse.

# Baby Wrapped in Quilt

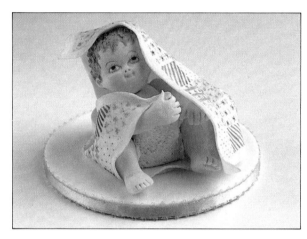

### Head
Make baby's head by pushing a large ball of skin-coloured paste into a plaster mould (made from cutting a small doll's head in half and making the impression). Place on a cocktail stick to dry.

### Body
Make a large cone, bend the cone slightly backwards and exaggerate abdomen. Create a curve between the back and bottom using forefinger. Make an indentation with a large ball tool where head, arms and legs are to be placed.

### Hands and Arms
Tap one end of a sausage and flatten to form a spade shape. Cut out a small 'V' for the thumb then cut fingers. Separate each finger, smooth and round tips. Place onto a piece of foam and curve fingers by drawing a ball

tool over them towards the palm, indent palm with ball tool. Form wrist, elbow and upper arm by rolling paste with fingers. Place in a natural pose to dry.

### Legs
Taper one end of a sausage and flatten to form a spade shape as for arms. Make 4 cuts for toes, round ends. Form heel and ankle using thumb and forefinger. Shape knee and thigh. Indent bottom of foot to create arch. Place in a natural position and dry.

### To Assemble
Attach head to body, and legs to torso. Make a nappy by rolling a piece of white paste to medium thickness and wrap around body. Texture nappy by pinching paste with fine pointed tweezers to create a towelling-like effect. Attach arms.

Pipe on hair using royal icing. Paint facial features and dust cheeks.

### Quilt
Position baby on a tissue paper template and practise wrapping baby in tissue until satisfied with folds, shape and lay the quilt so that when the baby is wrapped in the actual paste it can be handled as little as possible as over handling and re-wrapping will cause the paste to crack and tear. When satisfied, mark on template the position of the baby's bottom. When the quilt is completely dry, paint in the patchwork pattern with a fine brush using clear paste colours. If working with more than one colour on each pattern, allow each colour to dry thoroughly or streaking will occur. Keep the brush as dry as possible, over-wetting of the paste will cause it to disintegrate.

# Koala
# in Tree

Make a wire support for the tree using heavy-gauge wire. Make two circular bases, wrap together with a finer-gauge wire, twist wire together to form a trunk. Divide into a fork shape. Add finer-gauge wire near the top of the tree for smaller branches. Colour gelatine paste brown. Build up the trunk with pieces of paste pushed into the wire, becoming thinner where the branches fork, leave to dry. Pipe royal icing over the shape and brush with a dry brush to create a textured finish.

## Koala
Make a greyish brown-coloured paste. Make a conical shape for the body. Tilt to one side slightly. Make a round shape for the face. Pinch out the nose until it protrudes, pinch together slightly to narrow. The face tends to be fairly flat and the eyes are quite far apart and quite small. Indent eyes with a small modelling tool. Make ears as for mouse but attach sideways into the head.

Attach head to the front of the cone, not the top. Smooth edges together with a modelling tool. Fix to tree at this stage with royal icing while the koala is still fairly moveable so that the branch indents the front of the koala and it fits snugly into the fork of the tree. It will then appear to be clinging to the tree and not simply placed on it.

## Arms and Legs
The thumb on the paw is fairly high up so make the first cut higher than usual. Make three further cuts for the other four digits. The wrist and arm are quite thick so only shape the wrist slightly. Repeat for the back legs but leave larger pieces of paste for the haunches. Attach limbs to koala so that it appears to be clinging to the tree itself.

Texture fur with royal icing and a dry brush. Make some eucalyptus leaves and attach to hand. Pipe in black eyes, glaze nose and when dry, glaze eyes.

# Skunk

### Head and Body

Make a cone shape, uptilt snout. Indent eyes with a small ball tool. Make a large flattened sausage for the body. Cut a large insertion and divide for legs. Smooth and round each leg. Insert a long wooden skewer into body to support it while dressing. Insert half a cocktail stick into each ankle, allow to dry thoroughly.

### Clothes

Make a normal frill for each ankle. Thinly roll out pink paste and using the pattern, cut out the skirt, smooth with large ball tool and thin all cut edges. Slightly frill bottom hem of skirt with ball tool. Wrap around the body. Place the seam at the front of the figure where it will be hidden by the apron. Smooth seam with finger to hide join as much as possible. Cut apron skirt in white paste and attach over the pink skirt with the opening at the back of the figure. Cut back and front bodice shapes and attach to the body. Indent with No1 tube and pipe bottom edge of bodice and around neck for a fine lace effect. Make two arms from black paste as for mouse. When dry, wrap sleeve around arm. Cut away excess paste on the inside at the top of the arm.

### Boots

Using black paste, make a sausage shape, bend for the ankle. Flatten bottom of boot, form a heel by moulding with forefinger. Glue and push onto cocktail stick.

### Tail

With white gelatine paste, make a tail. Roll a sausage long enough to place up inside the skirt. One end should be fairly narrow, it should be thicker in the middle with a thick end to attach to the body. Support each end with foam to lift while drying.

# Teddy Birthday Plaque

Make rounded cone shape for body and insert cocktail sticks where head, arms and legs will be positioned. Texture body by pinching the paste with fine pointed tweezers. Make the head quite large in proportion to the rest of the body. Make a tall pinch one side of the ball to form snout, indent eyes with ball tool. Make ears as for mouse, and attach to head, texture as before.

## Legs and Arms
Make a large cone for each arm, pull out pointed end and flatten to form paw. Shape wrist by rolling fingers, texture and place in a curved position to dry. For each leg, make a large cone, flatten and pull out as for arm to form foot, bend at the knee and leave a large piece of paste for haunch; texture. Note: Place both arms and legs onto body before drying so that the cocktail sticks inserted into torso will

form a hole in the limbs. Support with foam when drying then attach to body with royal icing. Attach head.

## Honey Pot
Make a flattened barrel shape. Roll a fine sausage. Join ends to form a ring. Place on top of barrel. Make a label from finely rolled white paste cut into a rectangle when dry, paint in 'HONEY'.

## Wrapping Paper
Roll out a piece of blue paste quite finely. Roll out a piece of white paste to the same thickness. Place one piece of paste over the other and roll together to form one piece of paste. Cut some small shapes using a plunger cutter and place on blue paste, these could be in a contrasting colour. Roll again to form one piece of paste. Cut into a square shape, roll up and lift or bend down corners to give a natural effect, support

until dry. Make a small birthday card by cutting a rectangular shape in white paste, fold in half and leave to dry. Paint message inside and design on front of card.

## Bee
Make two balls of paste one yellow and one black. Slice each ball into sections. Reassemble to form a ball of alternative colours. Make a ball for the head, insert two stamens for antennae. Roll black paste finely into strands, bend to form legs. When dry, attach to body with royal icing.

## Wings
Use a small rose petal cutter. Cut two wings, dry. Paint veins; dust with gold sparkle. Wings can either be attached to the body with royal icing when both are dry or the dry wings can be inserted into the body while the paste is still soft.

# Clown Jack-in-the-box

### To Assemble
Make ribbons and place into plaque. Place wrapping paper on top of ribbons. Place honey jar on paper. Fill pot with honey-coloured icing made to runout consistency, allow to drip down the side of the jar and onto the paper. Position teddy, bee and card.

## Clown Jack-in-the-box

### Spring
Make a spring by wrapping a heavy gauge wire around a round pencil, remove and screw into body shape. Push a perspex tube up through the spring and push into the body, dry.

### Face
Make a ball of skin-coloured paste. Roll to form neck, roll and push finger into paste to form a chin.

Cut out two white ovals for the eyes and curved half moon for the mouth. Indent with a ball tool for nose. Paint on features with black and red paint, add a red ball of paste to nose indentation. Glaze nose with gum arabic glue or confectioner's glaze.

### Clothes
Make a fairly rough body. Using pattern cut out T-shirt. Place on the body, create creases and folds in the paste. When dry, paint on the stripes. Cut a long strip of red paste, wrap around the waist area for the trousers. To create a baggy effect, pull down and stretch edge with finger and thumb. Cut two thin strips for braces. Make two buttons by rolling two small balls of cream paste, flatten and indent a circle with a large icing tube, make two holes to create a shank with a large needle.

Cut out jacket-fronts. Smooth cut edge with a large ball tool. Shape bottom edge to create a natural effect. Cut out back of jacket and glue in place. Cut two lapels. Ball to slightly frill cut edge. Roll and form lapels, again to create a natural effect.

### Heads and Arms
Make a long sausage for the arm, bend and leave to dry. To make a wrist shape, make a cone of skin-coloured paste, push a cocktail stick into the paste and taper the end; leave to dry. Push the wrist shape into the arm, leave to dry.

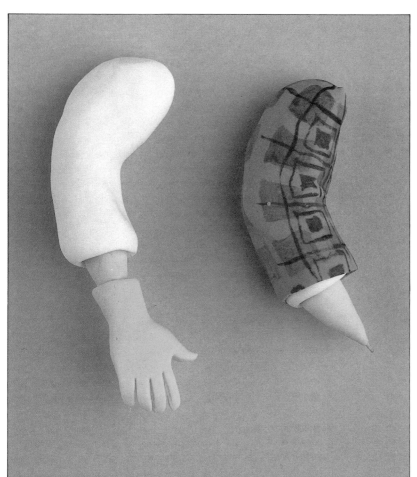

## Glove

Make a hand as for the baby. Extend the wrist to push a piece of dowelling the end of the glove and open up the paste. Cut a V section from the cuff. Roll edge to thin, push onto wrist shape. Before covering the arm with a sleeve, decide on the position of the arms so that the sleeve seam is placed where it will be less visible, either on underside or inside the arm. Paint the check pattern on the jacket. Make hair by pushing some soft paste through a clay gun or a garlic press, attach to head.

## Bow Tie

Roll out some green paste, make small balls of red paste and push these into green paste, re-roll paste and cut out the shape using the pattern. Pull the tie ends towards the middle and glue. Wrap a small strip of paste around centre of bow. Glue in place at the neck.

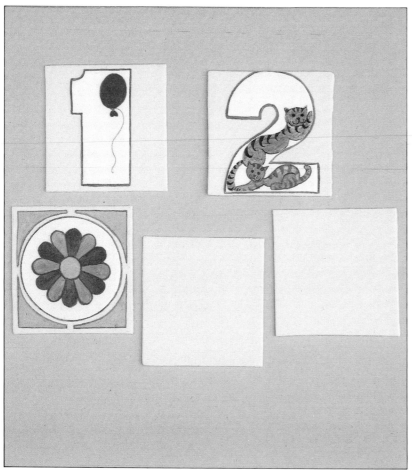

## Box

Roll out pale yellow paste to medium thickness, using template cut five squares. When dry, paint a design, letter or number on each square. If numbers are chosen, the age of the child could be on the front of the box.

**To Assemble**
Pipe royal icing on edges of square, butt edges together. Support until dry. Assemble three sides. Push clown on perspex rod into cake. Place three box sides around clown, attach fourth side and lid. Make beach ball from gelatine paste and paint when dry. Make a small rag doll or teddy, prop against ball. Attach ribbons to cake in colours to match clown.

Trousers –
Cut one

Bow Tie – Cut one

Face

Vest – Cut one

Jacket Back – Cut one

Sleeve – Cut two

Lapel – Cut two

Jacket Front
– Cut two

Jack in the Box

Bramble

Dress Bodice – Cut one

Apron Rib – Cut one

Apron Bow – Cut one

Sleeve – Cut two

Apron Skirt – Cut one

Skirt – Cut one

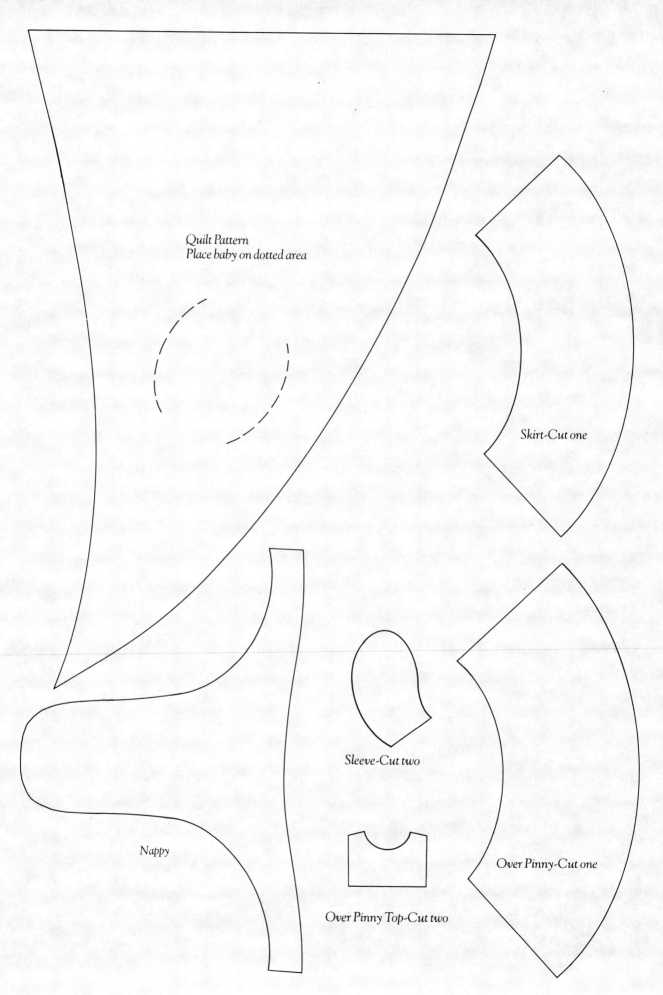

Quilt Pattern
Place baby on dotted area

Skirt-Cut one

Sleeve-Cut two

Over Pinny-Cut one

Nappy

Over Pinny Top-Cut two

# Tube Embroidery and Broderie Anglaise

# Iced Embroidery

Embroidery designs of all kinds are very easily adapted for use as cake decorations. This involves piping the individual 'stitches' with a fine icing tube using fairly soft icing.

Embroidery refers to both large complex designs using several colours and also to the fine lacy embroidery motifs commonly used for side decoration which are generally piped in one colour. This method allows the decorator endless scope as it can be effectively used for a variety of designs including symmetrical patterns, floral, figures, crests and lettering.

Once you have practised the stitches, any embroidery pattern can be used as a guide. Fabrics, wall coverings and even some china will give many lovely designs which may inspire you to create patterns.

Before starting a design, mix up all the colours and shades of icing which you will be needing. Put a small amount of all the colours in piping bags with a No 0 tube. Use small bags and do not more than half fill them, this allows you more freedom of movement and is more accurate as you will be working closer to the design.

Start working the design beginning with the background, working towards the front. Complete one section at a time, changing the shade where necessary before starting another part of the design. For

example, a petal may be pale at the tip darkening towards the base, therefore, the pale tip should be piped first. While this is still wet, change to a darker colour and carry on piping all in one operation. This will produce a smooth result and the shades will blend well. A fine, slightly damp brush should be drawn through the stitches if they look uneven and any little peaks should be flattened while still wet. If some parts need special emphasis, they may be built up slightly by using extra pressure.

62

# Marking out the Design

## Pricking

Trace the design onto tracing paper. Place this on the cake or plaque and carefully prick the outline with a pin. Do not mark too many details as this will be confusing and these small features can easily be copied when the design is almost finished. This method is not suitable for hard surfaces.

## Pencil Tracing

The usual method of tracing is to turn over the design, re-draw on the back with a sugarcraft pen, or with non-toxic pastel pencil, place this side on the surface to be decorated and trace again over the outline. This leaves the fine lines of the pattern on the surface. Do not use very heavy lines as these will be difficult to conceal and could smudge. Small pieces of outline embroidery which are mainly used to decorate the sides of a cake or scattered around a large decoration to give a softening effect are usually done freehand with a No0 or 00 tube. The focal points of the design may be pricked out with a pin, this will ensure that the side motifs look uniform even though there may be some slight variations. The icing nozzle should gently scrape the surface as the icing is squeezed out using an even pressure and should be held rather like a pen. Fresh soft icing which has been well beaten should be used, this should flow easily without needing too much pressure.

# Embroidery Stitches

## 1. Long and Short Stitch

Is used to fill a large shape with an arrangement of stitches blended to create a smooth surface. Pipe a fine outline. First row, make long and short stitches. Second and successive rows, the stitches are all the same length. The last rows need tidying up so another row of long and short will fill the spaces left. The direction of stitches should follow the lines of the design.

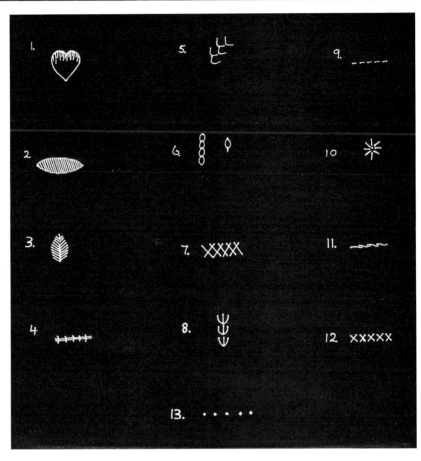

## 2. Satin Stitch

These are straight stitches, worked together to form a band or shape and are used for small or narrow shapes.

## 3. Fishbone Stitch

Made up of lines piped diagonally towards the centre and repeated the other side in reverse direction. Useful for leaves or feathers.

## 4. Couching

One or more threads are laid down and stitched into position. This can be used where a very bold outline is required. This stitch is used by embroiderers when they are using metallic threads like gold or silver and would be appropriate in oriental designs.

## 5. Feather Stitch

Pipe a U shape with the next one starting below and to the centre of the first stitch.

## 6. Chain Stitch

A row of chains makes an interesting outline and can be used for stems. A long chain stitch worked singly is known as a lazy-daisy stitch and is used for small flower petals.

## 7. Herringbone Stitch

A series of diagonal lines overlapping at the top and the base.

## 8. Fern Stitch

A simple arrangement of three stitches worked at angles to each other. Useful for grasses or leaf veins.

## 9. Running Stitch

Short straight stitches with a gap between them. Useful for outlining or for filling shapes when a very light effect is required.

## 10. Star Stitch

Straight stitches radiating from a central point.

## 11. Stem Stitch

Used for stems and outlines.

## 12. Cross Stitch

The traditional stitch for samplers. Used for outlines, fillings and borders.

## 13. French Knots

Pipe a tiny bulb of icing. Used for stamens or decorative fillings.

# Tube
# Embroidery

**1.** Outline of the design is embossed onto the soft sugarpaste.

**2.** Stems and leaves which lie behind the flower are completed. Leaves in chain stitch and stems in stem stitch.

**3.** First part of the petal completed with long and short stitches using pale pink.

**4.** Centre of the petal completed in darker colour and blended at the change-over point. Complete petals at the back first.

**5.** Design is completed by adding the petals which appear to be in front. The centre is piped in black satin stitch and stamens around the edge are French Knots.

Harebells worked in long and short stitch.

Crewel work lilies.

Pansies worked in long and short stitch.

Crewel work floral plaque.

# Broderie Anglaise

This is also known as eyelet, Madeira or Swiss work. Designs usually consist of simple floral motifs as the round and oval holes lend themselves so well to floral formations. Work on fresh soft sugarpaste.

Prick out focal points with a pin. Take care when pricking designs not to lean hand on the surface of the paste as this will spoil a good finish. Round holes are made by holding a paintbrush handle or knitting needle (pin) at right angles to the cake and pressing gently into the paste.

Oval holes are made by holding the same tool at 45°, this will make an elongated hole. Pipe around all holes with a No 0 tube. To give a perfectly round circle, outline half the hole in a clockwise direction then pipe the other half in reverse direction. Neaten the take-off point with a damp brush if necessary. Traditional broderie anglaise has a scalloped edge which is sewn with buttonhole stitch. This effect can be achieved by piping a small open zig-zag.

**1.** Design pricked out through the pattern with a pin.

**2.** Holes are made with paintbrush handle.

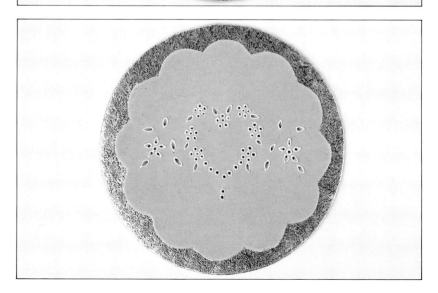

**3.** All holes are outlined with a No 0 icing tube.

**4.** Fine lines and dots are piped in to complete pattern.

**5.** Edge is worked in a zig-zag to represent buttonhole stitch.

# Lazy Daisy Cake

Coat a 28cm (11in) round board with coloured sugarpaste. Cut a scalloped template from a 28cm (11in) circle by folding into 16 sections and cutting about 1cm (½in) away from the edge of the pattern to form a curve.

Roll out white sugarpaste quite thinly. Cut scalloped shape and carefully lift onto the board. Mark the main holes for broderie anglaise using pattern as a guide. This process should be completed before the cake is placed on the board as it will be easier to make the holes.

Cover the cake with coloured sugarpaste. Gently lift into the centre of the board and secure with icing. Make a small scalloped shape for the top using same method as before, the finished shape should be about 2.5cm (1in) smaller than the diameter of the cake and should also have 16 scallops.

Mark out the pattern and make the main holes. By pressing right through to the coloured paste, the deeper colour will show through enough to make a better contrast. Care should be taken not to press into the cake itself as this will cause a dark stain to gradually seep through to the surface.

Outline all the holes on the board and the top of the cake and pipe in fine embroidery. Edge stitch scallops using zig-zag lines. Make a template for side decoration, using a strip of paper to fit the side of the cake. Cut shape from the guide. Attach to the cake and mark out the pattern. With cake tilted away from you, pipe the curved lines. Pipe daisy decoration. Pipe snailstrail around the base of the cake. Attach bands of ribbon around base and make small bows using two colours of ribbon together. Add top decoration of flowers or an ornament to suit the occasion.

*Templates for designs illustrated in this lesson*

71

*Templates for designs used in this lesson*

# Brush Embroidery

# Brush Embroidery

$T$his is a versatile technique whereby the decorator can produce attractive designs quite simply and quickly. If a little more time is taken for highlighting and shading the design, the same method can be employed to create a beautiful, delicate finish.

A white design on a white background which would be most suitable for a wedding cake makes a very elegant decoration and brush embroidery would be a good technique for reproducing the design of the bridal lace. Although the pattern is not very clearly defined it will show up quite well by contrast of light and shade.

A more dramatic effect will be achieved by piping a white design on a dark background, or a dark brown design on a cream background. In this case the pattern is defined by varying the density of the icing and brushing in the direction of the natural veining of petals and leaves. However, the most beautiful designs are those in which several complementary colours are used and delicately highlighted with diluted food colouring after the icing has completely dried.

# Transfer of Design

On soft, fresh sugarpaste it is best to emboss the design by placing the pattern under a piece of perspex or glass which should be larger than the top of the cake so that the surface will not be marked by the edge of the perspex. If glass is used it should be bound with strong tape to prevent cuts.

Outline the design by piping on top of the perspex with a No 0 or 1 tube and white icing made without glycerine. Do not pipe in small details as these can be added later. Allow to dry thoroughly. This method will produce a reverse image and if this is undesirable, the design should be turned over and re-traced on the back before placing under the perspex.

## Pencil Transfer

This method, which seems to be popular, should be very carefully worked, as a mistake will result in a dark line in the wrong place which may be very difficult to conceal.

Trace over the pattern with tracing paper and a medium hard pencil to give a clear, sharp line. Turn over tracing paper and re-trace the pattern with a non-toxic pencil or pastel. Place this side on the cake and using a smooth tip such as a ball point, lightly trace on to the cake.

This method is useful where the design of the top continues over the side of the cake. The icing should be allowed to harden for a few days before tracing to avoid making pit marks.

## Pricking

This is only suitable for very simple designs or freehand work where it is only necessary to mark positions of small decorations, as the result may not be clearly enough defined for accuracy. It is not a very successful method for use on hard icing.

## Materials

A No1 tube is used for most designs but where the work is very small and a large build-up of icing is undesirable, a No 0 should be used. Choose a good quality sable brush as this will be firm and springy and will give better results than a cheap brush with weak bristles. Use a No2 or 3 for brushing the icing and highlighting and a 2/0 or 3/0 for adding fine detail.

Use fairly soft, fresh royal icing or, if you need longer to work on the design before it dries out, add about one teaspoon of clear piping gel to every four tablespoons of icing. The gel is seldom necessary, so try working without it and then compare the results when the gel is added.

## Working Brush Embroidery

When preparing to start a multi-coloured design, fill several small icing bags containing a No 0 or 1 tube with all of the colours you intend to use. As this entails using a lot of expensive tubes you can try using a firm bag without a tube and carefully snipping off the end of the bag after filling it to form a tiny hole about the size of a No1 tube. The bag must be changed as soon as the hole becomes distorted. Keep your colours quite pale as they can be emphasised where necessary by touching up when the work is finished.

Work from the outside of the design towards the centre, dealing with the background first and working on only one small section at a time. The background should be light and delicate so that it will not over-power the detail in the foreground.

The paintbrush should be damp. If it is too dry the icing will become rough and uneven. If it is too wet it will make a puddle which will spoil the surface of the cake. The brush should be held at an angle of 45° and long strokes should be used which start at the edge of the petal or leaf and continue to the base to avoid ridges.

Pipe a line around a leaf in the background then, before the icing dries, quickly pipe another line within. Using long smooth strokes, brush the icing through both lines towards the base, leaving more icing at the edge of the leaf and fading away to a thin film at the base. Where the leaf is serrated, it is more satisfactory to pipe a small blob of icing at each point within the outline instead of a continuous line. Take care to conceal transfer lines with your outline and to brush the icing in the direction of the natural veining on petals and leaves.

As you are brushing from the background towards the front, a little icing may be inadvertently brushed on to the area immediately in front of the part on which you are working. This is not important if it is only a light film of icing, as this will be covered when that section is outlined and brushed.

The flowers in a design are usually in front of the leaves and the back petals should be done first so that the front petals will be emphasised. The furled edges of a flower should be left until last and completed by piping a heavy line all around it and infilling with icing. Light brushing with a damp brush will smooth the area. Finally pipe in any stamens. Leaf veins can be defined by either brushing away the wet icing or by piping them in with a very fine tube.

Shadows and highlights should be painted in when the icing is completely dry, using as little moisture as possible. Water may be used to dilute the food colouring but care should be taken not to get the icing too wet. A spirit such as gin or vodka is preferable as this will dry immediately. Before brushing the colour onto the icing, try it out on a spare piece of icing as the wrong colour will be impossible to remove. To take away the flat look from a leaf, brush one side darker and always darken the same side to show that the light is coming from one direction. The base of a petal will be a deeper colour than the tip. Use an almost dry brush and very light strokes to obtain subtle shading.

# Working Brush Embroidery

**1.** Mark out design by embossing or tracing.

**2.** Outline leaves in the background. Pipe inner line, complete each section first. Brush through from tip to base with long smooth strokes using a damp brush.

**3.** Pipe and brush through leaves in the foreground. Pipe in calyx of bud.

**4.** Brush flower petals leaving furled edge.

**5.** Pipe furled edge of petals with heavier line, smooth with damp brush and add details.

# Magnolia Cake

Cover cake with sugarpaste. Cut a template to fit the side of the cake, mark into 6 or 8 sections and cut into a scalloped shape. Mark line of scallop onto the side of the cake with a scriber. Transfer the magnolia design by embossing or tracing. Mark side motif in each scallop. Pipe fine snailstrail around the cake base.

Complete brush embroidery on top of the cake. Tilt cake away from you for side embroidery, which is easier if done at eye level.

Make flounce using a circular frill cutter. To layer the flounce at the points, cut circles into three equal sections, frill and stick by brushing the unfrilled edge with water. Stick each piece to the cake below each point at board level adjusting the frill as you go. For the second layer, cut each circle into four equal pieces and repeat the procedure, sticking each piece above the first layer. A third layer can be used, but if the top edge extends beyond the marked scallop line, this must be carefully cut away with a scalpel.

For the top flounce, cut circle of paste and open out. Frill one edge and cut to fit the scallop. Stick to the cake, adjusting frill and neatening the top edge. Repeat all around cake, tucking in ends of the frill at the points. Finally, pipe a fine edging around top of the flounce to disguise the join.

Magnolia Cake

# Lace

# Lacing

Fine lace makes the most beautiful and delicate decoration which has always been prized for adding a touch of elegance to a garment, raising it above the ordinary level.

In recent years there has been a revival of interest in lace-making as a craft and of course, it has always been popular for wedding dresses. It follows naturally that lace work is also a very popular form of cake decoration, since the addition of finely piped lace will add delicacy to many designs. Although it is very fragile, when it is made correctly, it is quite easy to apply to the cake and transport without breakage. Small lace pieces are commonly used as an edging above a border of extension work or flounces, to add interest to a row of ribbon inserts, or to surround a picture or floral arrangement on top of a cake. Larger pieces can be placed close together around the base of a cake at an angle of 45°, taking the place of a flounce or extension work.

The icing must be very strong and you will have more success by using egg white in icing for this work.

## Designing Lace
To design pieces of lace, draw the shape of one side quite roughly. Lay a piece of tracing paper over this shape and improve on it in pencil, altering the lines until you are satisfied with the shape. Fold the tracing paper in half and trace off the other side which should match perfectly.

### EQUIPMENT
Waxed paper or baking parchment
or
thick transparent plastic sheet.
Several icing tubes (preferably No 00 or 0 for delicate lace). No 1 can be used for outlining large pieces.

# Method of Work

### Method

Tape the pattern to the flat board and stick the wax paper on top with dots of icing.

To pipe small lace pieces, take a 00 or 0 tube and a small paper bag. Put only a little icing in the bag. For lace which consists of small curves, the bag should be held rather as you would hold a pen, with the tube close to the pattern. Pipe over the design, but do not actually scrape the surface. Even pressure is very important – too much pressure will cause uneven lines, too little pressure will produce weak spots which will be easily broken. It is important that all the lines of the lace touch as any gap will make it weak. Pipe many more pieces than you need to allow for breakages. Leave to dry. To remove, slip the palette knife underneath to free it or loosen with a dry paintbrush. To attach to the cake, pipe a few dots of icing where the lace is required, gently touch the lace to the icing and position at 45°.

### Care of Equipment

Fine tubes will easily become blocked even when the sugar is finely sieved so it is best to avoid wearing fluffy sweaters or to wear an overall with sleeves and to keep the icing covered at all times.

If the tube should block, put it to soak and later clean it with a small brush. Fill another bag with fresh icing. Never try to clear a tube with a pin as it could damage the end of the tube.

### Storage

To store any lace which is not required, leave on the wax paper and lay flat in a box with a lid. As sugar absorbs moisture, any humidity in the air will cause the icing to soften, therefore, it must be kept in a dry cupboard or the box should contain some silica gel crystals which are available from chemists. The self-indicating variety change colour when they become damp and should be dried out in the oven.

### Colouring Lace

Sometimes it is necessary to colour lace to match ribbons or flowers. If you decide to tint the icing before piping, it would be better to use liquid colouring for this purpose as most paste colours contain glycerine which will soften the icing. Another method is to pipe the lace in white and when dry and still attached to the wax paper, brush lightly with petal dust mixed with a little icing sugar.

### Large Lace Pieces

These should be piped with a fine tube for a delicate effect but the outline may be piped with a No1 tube to add strengh. Another way of strengthening a large piece of lace is to turn it over by slipping an artist's palette knife underneath the icing to remove it from the wax paper, or by drawing it to the edge of a table and letting it protrude a little over the edge, at the same time gently peeling away the paper, supporting it well all the time. When the lace is turned over, pipe another line on the back of the outline and leave to dry.

### Lace Piped on Net

Some of the finest needlepoint and bobbin lace in the world is embroidered or appliquéd on to a fine net base. It is possible to create a very authentic effect by piping a lace design on to a net base. This is a very practical method for making a deep lace border.

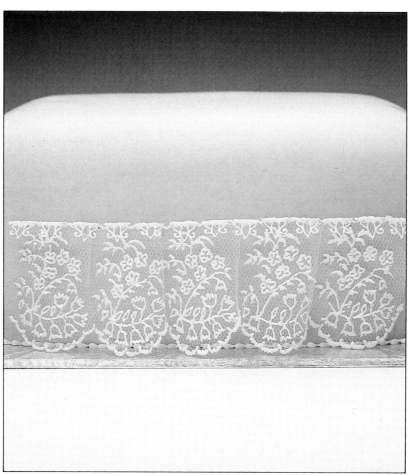

# Border 1

Cut a strip of fine net deeper than the motif. Place the pattern on a board, cover with transparent plastic film and stick the net on top with dots of icing or pins if the board is suitable. The icing should be quite soft for this as it will break away from the net if it is too stiff, but it will need to be firm enough to hold its shape. Pipe the pattern as many times as the strip requires including the scalloped edge. When dry, cut the edge close to the scallops with small pointed scissors. This border has small pleats between motifs to give fullness. These should be stitched to hold in place. The net should be bent over the finger to take away the stiffness. This will enable it to flounce nicely. Pin the completed strip to the cake and pipe a neat line to secure the net to the cake. Remove pins when dry. Small pieces of lace make a pretty edge to hide the join.

# Border 2

This border is piped the same way and is applied straight to the cake by piping with royal icing and attaching separately piped lace pieces over the top edge of the cake.

## Floral Motif 1

Place wax or plastic film over the design and lay fine net on top. Using medium peak icing and 0 or 00 tube pipe all the outlines and fill in the solid areas. Dry for several hours. Using pointed scissors or a sharp scalpel, cut around the flower. These can be fixed to the cake using dots of icing or egg white.

## Floral Motif 2

The fuchsia motif is piped and cut out as before. It is then gently bent into a curve and pinned into place on the cake, then attached with small dots of icing. The pins are removed when the icing is dry.

# Side Decorations

## Side 1

Here small lace pieces are used to accentuate a heart shape which was scribed on to the side of the cake. The spotted decoration could be replaced with a monogram or floral design.

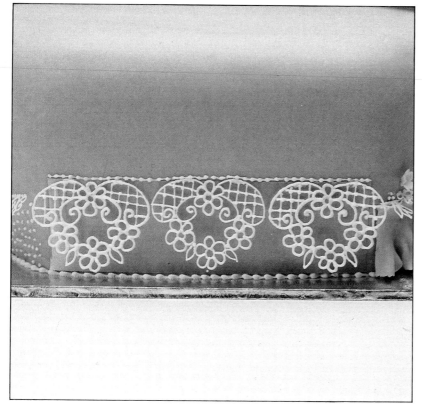

## Side 2

Larger pieces of lace attached to the top of a band of ribbon and left suspended. As they are a little heavier than the small pieces, they should be supported for a few minutes until the icing is able to hold them.

## Side 3

Two rows of lace are attached to the top of a straight flounce. The top row of lace pieces are smaller than the underneath row. Small plunger flowers are an added interest.

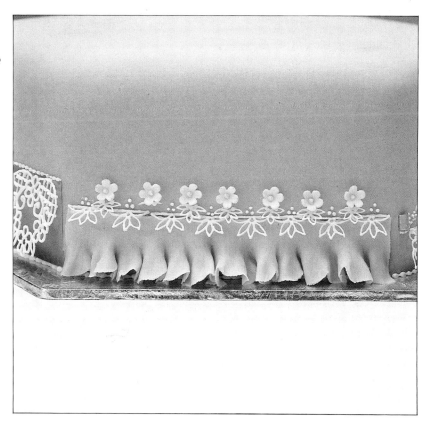

## Side 4

This side decoration is based on a band of ribbon at the centre with embroidery and lace above and below.

# Cockerel

This was piped on plastic film which had been taped over the design. All of the open areas must be filled in as illustrated to strengthen the figure. Dry well, remove from the film by drawing to the edge of the table and easing the film away. Care must be taken to support all parts with the hand. Attach to cake top with small dots of icing.

# Girl

Pipe as for the cockerel. All areas of the dress and apron must be filled in with piping. It is better to pipe the facial features and the hair directly onto the cake after the figure has been transferred into position.

# Blue Cake with Flounce

Pipe the figure of the little girl on wax paper using the pressure-piping technique, allow to dry. If you wish to inset the figure, cover the top of the cake with a disc of sugarpaste exactly the same size as the cake. Using a cutter or a template, cut out a circle large enough to take the figure. Now cover the cake in the normal way. Ease the paste around the cut out area and make a cut in the middle to make the shaping easier. When the covering is quite smooth, drop in a disc to fit the hole. Stick the figure in position with a little royal icing. Surround the inset figure with small pieces of lace standing upright. A double flounce around the base of the cake has the same lace as an edging trim.

The butterflies are piped on wax paper using a No 0 tube. They are piped in two colours and allowed to dry. Attach to the side of the cake with small dots of icing. The antennae must be piped directly on to the cake to avoid breakage. Use a dry paintbrush to help support this delicate lace.

A small posy of miniature flowers is placed off-centre. There is also room to pipe a name if appropriate.

*The cake is illustrated in full on page 84.*

*Starting with Scrolls*

*Starting with Half Circles*

*Arrangement of Petal Shapes*

*Variations on Hearts*

*Based on Oval Centre*

*Drawing a row of lace pieces onto squared paper or graph paper so that the pieces are all the same size.*

93

*Templates for Cockerel and Girl*

# Extension Work

# Extension Work

**E**xtension work or curtain work is a very delicate form of decoration. Simple extension work consists of a bridge which is formed by piping a series of dropped loops with subsequent rows piped exactly on top of the previous row.

The bridge supports very fine vertical lines which are piped from a straight or shaped line previously marked on the side of the cake and attached to the bridge at the base. Use a No 0 or 00 tube to achieve this fragile effect. Patience is needed to produce the neat, even finish which is essential in work of a high standard and the decorator should practise using a fine tube before attempting this work.

The extension work should be designed to complement the shape of the cake and any other decoration which is to be used. Therefore, all of the features on the cake must be planned together to make a balanced design. A narrow straight band of extension work will fit in with most cakes whatever their shape and size and will allow plenty of freedom to use lace, flower or embroidery work. An ornate section of perhaps tiered extension or overpiped extension work with a lace edging is an important feature on its own, and to show up its delicate beauty, the rest of the decoration should be simple.

If there is to be a straight band of ribbon above, the curtain work will look better if it has a straight top. If the top edge is to be shaped with points or scallops and decorated with lace, both should be worked out together to be sure that the lace is not too wide to fit small spaces. The extension work is not usually any deeper than one-third of the depth of the cake, otherwise it looks out of proportion. It is also more difficult to pipe very deep lines as the pull of gravity may cause threads to break.

Where there is to be a flower at the base of the cake or a very long spray trailing low over the side, the extension work could be designed in sections with a gap in the appropriate place or have high and low points so that the flowers could be positioned above the low point. A square or hexagonal cake is ideal for tiered extension work as this makes a very good corner design with two or three rows of extension work, one above the other at the corner tapering down to a single row in between. When

working out the design for a tiered cake, the same method is used for each cake regardless of size, the scallops will be the same width on each cake but the number will vary.

## Preparation

Before commencing the extension work, check that the coating of the cake is smooth and free of blemishes right down to the board as very fine work will not hide any major faults in the covering. Check that the sides of the cake are quite straight.

It is easier to pipe curtain work when the cake board is not too large but it must be large enough to protect the bridge from accidental knocks.

## Icing

Good extension work requires good quality icing which must be of the correct consistency, well beaten and free from lumps or specks which could block a fine tube. The addition of a little liquid glucose will give the icing more stretch, which is a great advantage when piping the fine vertical threads. Use 1ml (¼tsp) liquid glucose to each egg white used and stir into the finished icing. To make the icing stronger, the egg white may be left in a greasefree glass bowl for about 24 hours at room temperature. Sieve the icing sugar several times through a very fine sieve or clean nylon stocking. This is a very laborious task but well worth doing when it saves the frustration of blocked tubes. The icing should be smooth and beaten to medium peak. Experience will show what is the correct consistency, if it is too firm it will not flow easily from the tube but if too soft the drop threads will have a tendency to break.

## Templates

Decide on the type of extension work to be used and make a template from greaseproof (waxed) paper the same length as the circumference or one side of the cake.

Fold this strip in half and repeat several times until the section is the right width for the base scallop,

approximately 2.5 cm (1in). The top edge of the template should now be drawn and cut into the required shape. For a straight edge, decide the depth of the extension work and cut the template in a straight line. Hold the template firmly against the side of the cake or secure with sticky tape. Mark the line for the top edge with a needle or scriber. Mark the position for the base scallops by inserting a needle at each fold in the paper. Pipe a snailstrail or row of beads around the base of the cake with a No 0 or 1 tube.

## The Bridge

Put the cake on the turntable or elevate to eye level. Tilt the cake away from you and pipe dropped loops to form a bridge with a No 0 or 1 tube, using the pin marks as a guide to the high points of the scallops. These loops should not touch the board and should also be clear of the snailstrail, they should lie securely against the side of the cake. A second row of scallops is piped exactly on top of the first row and the bridge is built up in this way, drying each row thoroughly before another is piped, until approximately six rows have been piped with a No 1 tube or ten rows with a No 0 tube. There should be no gaps between the rows of scallops as this will make a weak bridge. If several rows are piped without drying each row, the whole bridge could sag or collapse. When the bridge is quite dry, the piping of the curtain work can be started.

Tilt the cake towards you to prevent the threads from sagging towards the cake. Commence piping straight lines by touching the tube to the marked top edge and squeezing out a thread which is then secured under the bridge. The next thread should be piped very close to the first. It is important that the spaces should not be wide enough for another thread to be fitted in between. Keep the bridge clean by wiping off any untidy ends with a damp brush. The threads must be piped straight and not leaning to either side, these should be checked every few inches and rectified if they are beginning to slope. If a tube gets blocked or the bag bursts, do not put the icing back in the bowl, discard and use fresh icing.

To finish the lower edge, one of the following methods may be used.

1. Pipe a dropped line with a fine tube, touching at the high point of the bridge and following the line of the bridge.
2. Pipe tiny loops at the base of the drop lines.
3. Pipe a row of tiny dots at the base of the drop lines following the line of the bridge. The top edge is neatened with finely piped dots or loops or lace pieces.

# The Bridge

## Plain extension work with a straight top.

This shows rows of bridge work piped one on top of another and the vertical lines piped from the top edge, over the bridge and secured underneath.

## Bevelled extension work.

This shows each row of bridge starting in the centre with a short line, a longer line is piped on top in the next row extending the same distance each side of the first line, each row is longer until the bridge covers the whole section.

## Overpiped extension.

Showing build up of the first bridge, the vertical drop lines and finally the second bridge with overpiped curtain effect.

## Upside-down bridge.

This is piped with the cake upside down.

## Basic Extension Work

Piped with No 0 tube and finished with drop loops and lace pieces.

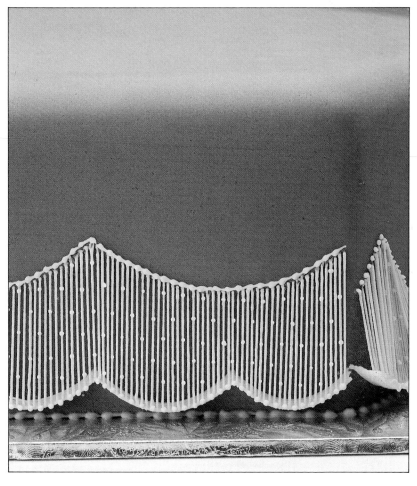

## Extension Work with a Shaped Top

The template is made by marking the base scallops as before and cutting the large scallop at the top, the width of two base scallops. Pipe the bridge and curtain work as before and finish by piping hailspots evenly over the surface. This must be done with a very light touch or the threads will break. The top edge is finished with a fine snailstrail and the bottom with more tiny dots.

## Overpiped Extension Work

The template is made as before but the top edge is cut into points, each one the same width as the base scallop. Pipe the usual way and allow to dry. The second bridge is piped exactly the same as the first and following the same lines. When all the rows are dry, the diagonal lines of the overpiping are done by tilting the cake to one side before piping in the direction the cake is leaning. Tilt the cake in the opposite direction to pipe the diagonal lines of the other side.

## Plain Extension with Ribbon Inserts

Narrow ribbon is let in at intervals by cutting the ribbon the same length as the piped lines and attaching with a dot of icing at the top and the bottom between each scallop. The top edge is finished with drop loops hanging away from the cake.

This is achieved by tilting the cake towards you very steeply, allowing gravity to pull the loops away from the cake. When the loops are dry, pipe tiny dots on them to decorate.

## Diagonal Overpiped Extension Work

This is a little more difficult and plain extension work should be perfected before attempting it.

Pipe the bridge as before and dry. Tilt the cake towards you and at the same time, put a prop underneath one side so that it is leaning sideways. This will allow the diagonal lines to hang straight. Pull out a strand of icing from the top line and attach it to a point on the bridge about 5mm (¼in) to the left or right of this point. Pipe all lines close together and evenly so that the angle remains the same all round. Dry. Remove the prop. Pipe a second bridge over the top of the first one. When this is dry, place the prop the other side of the cake then overpipe with diagonal lines in the opposite direction.

## Bevelled Extension Work

The base lines for this type of extension work are straight instead of scalloped. The first line is very short and centred between the section marks. The second row is piped on top and a little longer, extending the same distance either side of the first line. Each line of the bridge is piped a little longer and the last line extends across the whole section. The finished bridge is in the shape of a crescent. The dropped lines are then piped in the normal way.

## Tiered Extension Work

The illustration shows two tiers but three tiers can be used if the cake design requires it.

Mark the base scallops on the cake. At the same time mark another row of scallops at the height required. The top of the second tier is shaped to a point, but any shape may be used to suit the shape of the cake.

Pipe the first bridge and when dry pipe vertical lines all around the cake. The second bridge is made by dropping loops close to the top of the first layer of drop lines. Pipe several rows as before. Pipe drop lines from the top of the design to the bridge and finish off both bridges with dots.

## Extension Work with Arched Bridge

Mark the design using a template cut to the shape you require. To pipe the bridge, the cake must be inverted by placing a piece of perspex or a smooth board on top and turning the whole thing upside-down. The cake should be iced several days before this to allow the covering to set. Pipe the bridge in the usual way and when dry, turn the cake right-side-up and continue with the extension work.

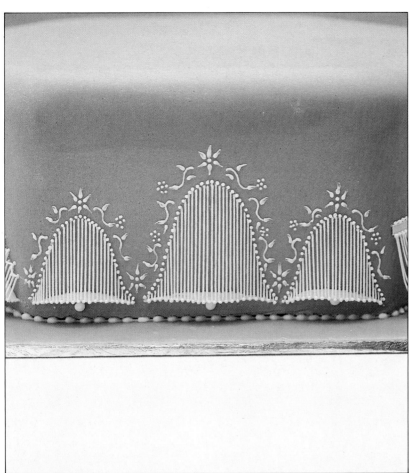

## Bells

Make a template in the shape of a bell and mark the design on the side of the cake. The bases of the bells are piped as for bevelled extension work but are slightly arched to give the appearance of a hollow bell. The cake should be turned upside-down for this part of the operation. The shape of the bell is piped by running drop lines from top to base, following the line of the bridge and this automatically forms the curve of the bell. Pipe a large bulb of icing at the base for the clanger.

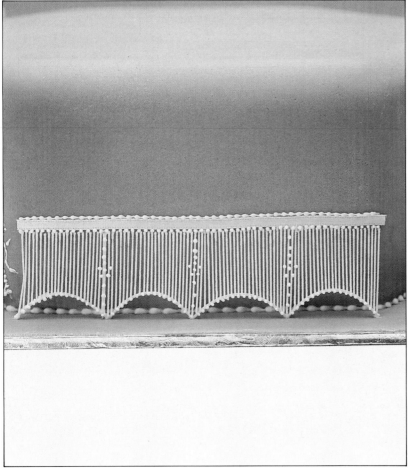

## Extension Work Suspended on Points

For this type of extension work, the board should first be covered with a thin layer of paste. The covered cake is placed in position and a fine snailstrail piped around the base of the cake. Using a template mark the place where the extension will touch the board, about 8mm (⅜in) away from the cake and the normal width for the scallops. Mark a straight line for the top. Turn the cake upside-down and elevate it so that the board surrounding the cake can be clearly seen. With No1 tube, pipe dropped loops from the board, suspending them from one mark to the next. Allow to dry for several hours before turning the cake upright. Leave until next day before piping the vertical lines. Pipe the fine threads from the top line and ending just below the arched loop which is standing on the board. Care should be taken not to knock these loops as they cannot be repaired unless the cake is turned upside-down again. When the drop threads are quite dry, pipe on decoration if required. Finish off the base of the drop threads with tiny dots. The top is also finished with dots, piped either side of a band of ribbon which was applied to the cake before the extension work was started.

# Bird Cake

This cake has the theme of birds running right through from the bird on the branch of blossom to the lace which represents feathers, down to the filigree birds which have been incorporated into the extension work.

The bird on the top was made by piping the basic shape minus the tail feathers, using the pressure piping technique. When dry, this was turned over and the same thing was piped on the back.

**Feathers**

These are made from thinly rolled flower paste. To apply the feathers, start from the tail. Cut out a template from the pattern and cut the individual feathers with a sharp knife. Curl them slightly by stroking along the length with a dog bone tool, starting at the top. While the feathers are still soft, stick to the body with a little egg white. Layer the feathers as in the pattern, working up to the body. Use bits of foam to support the curl of the feathers until they are dry. The body feathers are much smaller and a daisy cutter was used to cut out a basic shape from which individual petals were cut. These were then shredded with small scissors forming a fringe which was then stuck on, overlapping the tail feathers. Complete the body by sticking rows of these feathers slightly overlapping the previous row and work towards the head. Paint the eye and the beak with a fine brush. The background blossoms were piped freehand using the brush embroidery technique to create the illusion of the bird being surrounded by blossom, disappearing into the distance.

The hawthorn blossoms were made by making a tiny calyx, attaching a wire to which cotton stamens had been taped. Petals were cut with the smallest of the miniature rose cutters and arranged around the stamens as for the dog rose.

Cut leaves from template, shape, vein and attach wire. When dry, bind flowers and leaves to form a branch. Stick the bird in position using dots of icing. Lay the branch over the bird, securing with icing. Pipe little feet on the branch.

**Filigree Birds**

Place wax paper over the pattern, secure with small dots of icing, pipe with a 0 tube. The central flower and the neck may be overpiped to give extra strength. Pipe more than you need as they are extremely fragile.

**Extension Work**

Measure the circumference of the cake and cut a strip of greaseproof (waxed) paper to fit exactly. Fold into even sections until you have the desired width for scallops. Draw the shape required for the top, planning the low points so that they are the same height as the filigree birds. Using the template, mark the design on the cake. Pipe fine snailstrail with a No0 tube. Pipe bridgework with a No0 tube as previously described.

**Lace**

Pipe pieces of lace in the feather design making more than you need. For a delicate effect use a No00 tube.

Pipe extension work with a No00 tube, keeping the threads very close together. When dry, pipe dots across the bridge to neaten.

Remove filigree birds very carefully from the wax. A cranked artist's palette knife is useful for this purpose. The birds have to be leaned against the low areas of the extension work and secured with tiny dots of icing. A dry paintbrush is useful to help support the birds until the icing is dry enough to hold them.

Attach lace pieces with dots of icing of the same colour. Pipe a neat row of tiny dots just above in a slightly deeper colour than the main coating.

*Templates for designs used in this lesson*

# Creating Embroidery and Lace Designs

# Tube Embroidery

**E**mbroidery and lace are of great importance in the creation of a beautiful cake which will form the centre-piece of a wedding or other important occasion.

This has become such a popular form of cake decoration that the same designs appear with monotonous regularity and, whilst still being very skilful, are no longer remarkable.

Originality is all important in making an impact and, although you may have adapted the design from another source, your interpretation in sugar will make a fresh original design for your cakes. Instead of always copying designs from cake decorating books, it is exciting to look at other sources of inspiration such as dress embroidery, wrapping paper, cards and lace wedding veils.

The following examples have been taken from some of these sources.

## Bird and Floral Branch Plaque

This design was taken from a Chinese fringed stole. It is worked entirely in bands of satin stitch. The tracing was taken from a photograph and was very small. It was enlarged using the grid method then lightly traced onto the plaque using a non-toxic pencil. A larger version of this design would make a good top decoration for an embroidery enthusiast or perhaps for a man who considers sprays of flowers to be too effeminate for him.

## Toadstool Plaque

The toadstool caps are worked in long and short stitch, the stems and leaves in satin stitch, the blackberries and small stones are made up of French knots, the larger stones in satin stitch, grasses in feather stitch.

The background is piped first, gradually working to the front. Toadstool caps are done in one operation, changing the shade where necessary and brushing through to even up the stitches. This tablecloth design would be suitable for the top of a cake, or, if reduced in size, would work well as a side design.

## Honeysuckle Plaque

This honeysuckle design was taken from a blouse; the design was roughly traced by placing tracing paper on top of the fabric and tracing through. Using the blouse for reference, the lines were drawn over with a pen to make them clearer. The design did not need reducing or enlarging for this plaque. The embroidery was executed with satin stitch, stem stitch and French knots, using medium peak icing and No 0 tube.

## Broderie Anglaise

All of the pattern examples were taken from fabrics, tablecloths, handkerchiefs, table napkins and blouse collars. A complete tracing was done, as for the honeysuckle plaque. The tracing paper was placed on the plaque which had been left to dry for a few hours but was still soft enough not to craze when the holes were made. Focal points were pricked with a pin, the pattern was then removed then the holes made with a brush handle as in Lesson 5. The design was worked as in previous step-by-step instructions. Use the same method for transferring the design to the sides and top of a cake.

This border design is simply a series of motifs joined by a curved line, embellished with leaves. This border may be adapted for any size of cake, just add more flowers to each row until you have the correct size. Try using other motifs to make your own design.

# Brush Embroidery

## Rose Design

Taken from wrapping paper. The individual flowers were attractive but did not form a compact design suitable for a cake so they were traced off separately and re-grouped. Method of work as described in Lesson 6.

## Butterfly Plaque

Work the background first, then the flowers, finally the butterflies so they appear to be on top of the flowers.

## Freesia Plaque

These are straggly flowers and difficult to group tidily but they are much loved by many people and are useful because they fit into many colour schemes, growing as they do in such a variety of colours. Team brush embroidery with a few moulded freesias arranged at the base of the cake is demonstrated here.

# Enlarging or Reducing a Design

**1.** Trace the outline of the picture on to tracing paper then transfer the design to squared paper by inserting carbon paper or by rubbing soft pencil on to the back of the sheet. Draw a rectangle around the tracing.

**2.** Draw another rectangle smaller to fit the size of the design you want. Count the squares in the original grid and draw the same number of squares in the second rectangle. Carefully copy the design on to the new grid. It will help to make tiny marks on each square where the lines of the design cross it, then you can join up these lines.

**Method 2**
The quickest and simplest method of altering the size of the picture is by photocopying. Many of the modern machines will enlarge or reduce images and if you do not have access to photocopying facilities, some public libraries, colleges and large stores offer this service for a small fee.

# Creating Lace Designs

Some wedding dresses and veils have such beautiful embroidery that the bride may wish to make it part of the theme for the wedding and as the cake is an important part of the wedding breakfast and the bride will stand near to it, the cake decorator may be asked to incorporate the embroidery into the design of the cake.

The following examples of embroidery are taken from pieces of Nottingham lace and the designs were transferred from the fabric as follows: lay a clean piece of tracing paper over the design and lightly trace the main points of the pattern, taking care not to tear the paper and risk soiling the garment with pencil.

Keeping the fabric close at hand for reference, re-trace the main lines. Draw in the fine details. Reduce or enlarge the design as necessary.

Another method of transferring the design is by photographing the material, then trace the outlines from the photograph. White lace will photograph better when taken against a dark background.

It may be necessary to simplify the design as some lace embroidery has a random effect due to the way the threads are laid down and this could make your piping look untidy.

## Lace Plaques

These are piped with a No0 or No00 tube and would be suitable for the sides of a cake. You will see that the shapes have been modified in some cases to give clearer lines to pipe.

It is not usual to trace the complete lace design onto the sugarpaste surface. As this work must be very fine, there is a danger that pencil marks may show. The focal points of the design should be pricked out and the piping done freehand.

# Nottingham Lace Cake

The side decoration is adapted from a piece of ecru Nottingham lace. The main features of the lace are the type of flower, the criss-cross effect of the line of the stems and the colour. The inverted V shape is a perfect place for extension work.

Cover an 20cm (8in) hexagonal cake with sugarpaste which has been tinted by kneading into it egg yellow or tartrazine-free cream paste colouring and just a trace of black to soften the colour. Mix the colour first into a small piece of paste and when thoroughly mixed, add this in small portions to the main piece of paste and knead well. If the paste has become too soft after kneading, cover and allow to rest in the refrigerator for a short time to become more manageable. As the tinting may cause the paste to dry out a little, this should be used on the day it is coloured to avoid problems of crazing. Leave the iced cake to set for at least a day before transferring the design. Trace the design onto paper. Hold the pattern against one side of the hexagon. Prick out the main points.

Pipe snailstrail around the base of the cake with No1 tube. Tilt the cake away from you and with a No0 or No00 tube, pipe the embroidery before starting the extension work. Pipe lace pieces onto wax paper or clear baking parchment. Leave to dry thoroughly. Always pipe more pieces than you will need to allow for breakages. Pipe a few dots or a fine line above the extension work in the position where you want to attach the lace, gently touch the lace to the wet icing and check that each piece is in line. Finish the lower edge with small dots or scallops. Add an arrangement of flowers to suit the colour of the cake or to match the bridal flowers.

*See page 105 for illustration of completed cake.*

Lace Designs

Tube Embroidery

*Brush Embroidery*

*Tube Embroidery*

# Bas Relief
# and Smocking

# Bas Relief

Bas Relief is a form of three-dimensional modelling in which less than half of the true depth of the figure projects from the background. Throughout history it has been widely used as a surface decoration in pottery, woodcarving and sculpture.

More recently bas relief has been adapted for use in cake decorating, as sugarpaste has shown itself to be an excellent medium for this technique. Cake covering fondant should be used in preference to modelling paste as it remains soft, thus giving a longer working period, it will also be more palatable when the cake is eaten.

The design should be transferred to the cake or plaque using one of the methods used in Lessons 5 and 6. If there is to be a background to your picture, this should be completed by hand painting, outline piping or brush embroidery before the bas relief is started.

The paste should be rolled out to about 5mm (¼in) thick or even less if the figure is very small. With a sharp pointed knife, cut out the section which is to be executed in bas relief. Moisten the underside and stick to the cake within the outline already marked. Generally the contours of a figure can be defined quite well by depressing the low lying areas or those appearing behind but if you wish to emphasise an even more raised area, a small piece of paste may be slipped underneath before the figure is stuck down, then commence the modelling. If necessary, decoration can be applied to the modelled figure by piping or by using the appliqué method.

# Step-by-Step
# Bas Relief

**1.** Design transferred to plaque with scriber. (Icing should be left to harden for a few days before attempting this method).

**2.** Sections of design cut out, edges neatened.

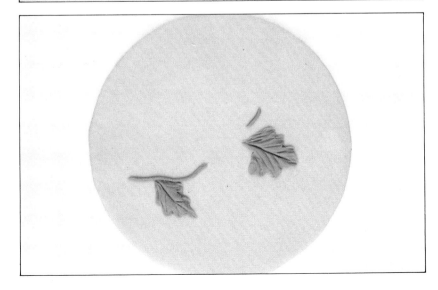

**3.** Parts appearing behind are worked first. Bevel edges with a divan tool and mark veins or any other definitions.

**4.** Add petals, bevel edges and mark petal veins.

**5.** Complete flower by adding the centre of the daisy and calyx. Prick the centre all over and pipe yellow dots around.

# Bas Relief

## *Plaques*

### Birds

The textures of the feathers are marked with a divan tool and the rounded body is emphasised by slipping a tiny piece of paste underneath. Smooth all the edges so that they almost blend into the background.

## Fish

This is an example of bas relief combined with appliqué. The weeds and fins are cut from modelling paste, shaped with a ball tool and applied to the surface before the body, which is decorated with piping and appliquéd bands of colour.

## Dutch Girl

The unclothed body and face were shaped with a divan tool. Extra care was taken when smoothing the face to avoid leaving any ridges. A pretty face is difficult to attain but keep the nose and chin small, trim the edge if it spreads too much, carry on smoothing and trimming until the result is pleasing to you. Arms and hands are applied after the dress. The cap is added last and decorated with cornelli work.

# Appliqué

**T**he technique of appliqué consists of applying cut-out shapes of material to the surface of other material, one shape can be laid on top of another to build up the picture.

In textile embroidery, felts are often used because they do not fray, whereas other woven materials have to be very carefully stitched to prevent fraying. The stitches most commonly used are straight overcasting and basic buttonhole stitch which serve the dual purpose of securing the shape to the foundation and preventing the pieces from fraying. In sugarcraft there are obviously no problems with fraying so the pieces can simply be stuck to the foundation. If the effect of embroidery is desired, a mock edging stitch can be piped around the pieces to complete the figure with one of the following stitches.

*Straight overcasting*

*Basic buttonhole stitch*

## Step-by-Step Appliqué (Lion)

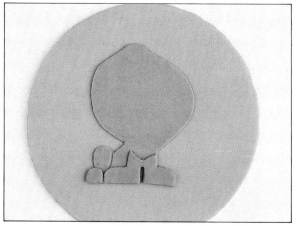

**1.** Body stuck to base. Legs moistened and laid in position on top.

**2.** Add mane and ears.

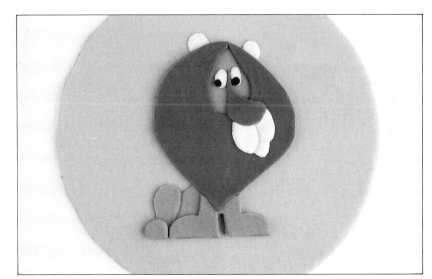

**3.** Add nose, eyes and muzzle.

**4.** Add black eyebrows, black nose and pupils of the eyes.

**5.** Paint black detail.

# Bells

The bells are cut from sugarpaste and the flowers and ribbons are made from finely rolled flower modelling paste. Flowers are shaped by pressing into a foam pad and completed with piped stamens. Decoration on bells is piped with No 0 tube.

# Bird

This is a good design for a child's cake. Any colours can be used to fit a theme. The small details are piped.

# Pink and White Floral Design

This consists of various shapes cut with petal and leaf cutters and laid out to form a pattern. Some of the petals have been cupped with a ball tool to add further interest.

# Smocking

Smocking is a technique traditionally applied to clothing and used for holding the fullness of the fabric in a decorative manner. Once the material is evenly gathered, a variety of stitches can be used for decoration

This method of smocking with sugarpaste is as near as possible to the conventional smocking of thin fabrics and its only function is that of decoration. It is a painstaking task as it must be neatly and evenly tucked but it forms a very attractive cake decoration.

---

### EQUIPMENT
Cake covering fondant mixed half and
half with flower modelling paste.
Cocktail sticks
Scalpel

---

### Method
To form the basic gathers, roll out the paste very thinly on a lightly cornfloured (cornstarched) surface. Cut a straight strip about 8cm (3in) deep and twice the width of the finished panel. If you require a very long strip to go all round a cake, this will have to be made up from several panels butted together.

Place one cocktail stick under the strip of paste making sure that it is straight, the next stick is laid on top, very close to the first. Carry on alternating the sticks, pressing them close until you have the width you want. Allow to set for about fifteen minutes.

Meanwhile, cut a strip of sugarpaste to the width and depth required for the finished panel. Remove the cocktail sticks and lay the ridged strip carefully on the moistened strip of the base. Adjust the gathers with a cocktail stick if they have become disarranged.

With a ruler and scalpel, using the minimum of pressure, cut the top and bottom edges straight. Panels should be arranged on the cake as soon as they are manageable, before they are completely dry. The panel is then ready to be embroidered in a variety of stitches.

Some of the traditional stitches pull and distort the tucks. If you wish to get this effect, plan the design and gently pull the tucks into shape before drying.

## Step-by-Step Smocking

**1.** Cocktail sticks placed alternately on top and underneath paste, pressed together to form folds.

**2.** Gathered strip of paste ready to be stuck onto base.

123

**3.** Gathers are stuck to the base and the top and bottom edge has been trimmed.

**4.** Smocking completed in a traditional design showing outline and trellis stitch. These stitches do not cause distortion so gathers have been allowed to remain straight.

**5.** The usual edge for smocking is a frill as this is naturally formed at the end of a band of smocking where the fullness of the material is released. Here a frill has been made and attached to the smocking. The join is overpiped with a smocking stitch.

# Stitches shown on Plaques

**1.** Vandyke Stitch.

**2.** Honeycomb Stitch.

**3.** Surface Honeycomb Stitch.

# Bird Cake

**T**his cake combines the techniques of bas relief and appliqué. The design was traced and transferred to the top of the cake.

The branch was piped first with No2 tube. The birds were cut from white sugarpaste, fixed in place and modelled by the bas relief method.

Any type of blossom cutter may be used for the flowers as long as it is large enough to be in scale with the rest of the picture. No attempt has been made to make the flowers realistic, the aim is to achieve an overall decorative effect. The flowers have been shaped by pushing them into a pad of foam and allowing them to set before sticking with a little royal icing. The birds were coloured by brushing lightly with black and blue blossom tint mixed together with cornflour (cornstarch) and wing and tail tips painted with diluted brown colouring. All the leaves were shaded with a darker green mixed with gum arabic liquid to give depth.

The base of the cake has a straight single flounce. Ivy leaves were attached in an irregular line and the stems piped in to finish.

*For illustration of the finished cake see page 115.*

Appliqué

Body

Mane

Eyebrows

Muzzle

Nose

Foot

Legs

Ears

Eyes

128

*Templates for designs illustrated in this lesson*

*Templates for designs illustrated in this lesson*

# Filigree

# Filigree

Filigree is a most useful form of decoration, which can be used to produce extremely intricate patterns. It can be used in its own right as a covering over a coated cake surface, or used to make a variety of models and decorations.

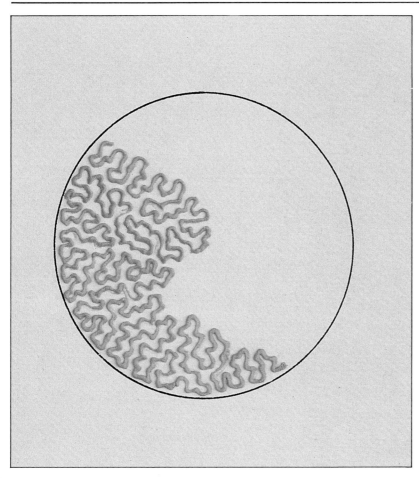

writing tube such as a No1 or No0. Hold the tube lightly against the surface to be decorated and apply pressure as for general piping work, then as you pipe, move the bag and tube from side to side and up and down to create a continual line of irregular shapes based on the letters 'm' and 'w' in a continuous string. Ideally when finished you should not be able to see the beginning and end of your piped line.

## Buttercream Filigree

Do not think of filigree as decoration produced with royal icing only. Buttercream is an ideal medium for piping filigree. The easiest way to apply buttercream filigree to a buttercream coated cake is to first chill the coated cake. This chilling will create a firmer surface on which to pipe. The cream used for piping can be warmed slightly in a bowl over warm water, this will help towards piping smoother lines. Use a No1 tube.

## Using Templates

Now cut out a simple template such as a crescent shape, use this for further practice. Templates can be very useful on actual cakes when piping filigree patterns, you can experiment with them on cake tops and sides to produce many interesting effects.

Filigree as its name suggests, should be fine, delicate and lace like. For this reason, filigree is normally executed using fine writing tubes No1, No0 and No00.

Use freshly made royal icing that has not been overbeaten, air bubbles can be a nuisance when piping with such fine tubes. Smooth the icing out using a palette knife on a clean flat surface, this will ensure the icing is lump-free. For shaped or formed filigree pieces, a pinch of cream of tartar in the icing will make a more solid finished item. If you intend to pipe filigree over shapes to be removed when dry, lightly grease the mould with a light white fat. The finished item can then be warmed gently to soften the grease and ensure an easy release.

Try to avoid making lace and filigree work on a damp, rainy day or in a steamy kitchen, the icing is so fine and fragile that any trace of moisture or humidity will hinder your work and delay the drying time of the icing. Remember also to take care to store the finished items in a dry place otherwise the filigree will collapse.

Probably the most difficult part of filigree work is removing the finished pieces from the waxed paper, so always make plenty of spares.

## Piping Filigree

An easy exercise to begin with is to draw out a shape such as a circle or a square onto thin card or a used cake board. Practise piping filigree using the outline as an edge to work to. Use coloured royal icing that will show up well and aid your practice. Use normal consistency royal icing and a fine

# Coffee Gateau

Coat a prepared cake in coffee-coloured and flavoured buttercream. The cake could be layered with coffee buttercream flavoured with a coffee-based liqueur such as Tia Maria. Comb scrape the sides of the cake, and decorate the base with plain shells piped in chocolate buttercream. Rest a strip of waxed paper onto the top of the chilled cream surface and pipe a straight line against it, remove the waxed paper. Use chocolate buttercream or piping chocolate (melted chocolate thickened with a few drops of cold water). Pipe the filigree in one half of the cake. Decorate the other half with small chocolate drops, made by piping melted chocolate onto waxed paper. A sugarpaste inscription plaque and some piped linework complete the gateau.

# Strawberry Cake

Prepare the cake by layering with strawberry-flavoured buttercream. Coat the cake in pink-coloured, strawberry-flavoured cream. Comb scrape the sides and chill the cake. Mark the cake top into four sections using the back of a knife. Place a food cutter in the centre of the cake and sprinkle some sieved jap biscuit crumb or fine nibbed nuts into the shape of the cutter, remove the cutter carefully. Next pipe straight lines of white buttercream using a 6mm (¼in) plain piping tube. The lines should start at the edge of the centre dressing and come out to the edge of the cake. Pipe filigree in the four sections, using pink buttercream. Now pipe a wavy line on the white buttercream lines using piping chocolate. Finish the top edge and the base with pink buttercream shells piped with a No44 tube. Model four strawberries from marzipan and mount them on discs of chocolate, piped onto waxed paper. Position the strawberry decorations on the cake.

# Filigree with Tulle

**F**iligree can be used to good effect when piped directly onto tulle. The tulle is so fine it becomes hardly noticeable against the piped filigree, but does help to keep the filigree together for shapes and formed filigree that would otherwise collapse.

## Filigree Casket

Using the templates provided at the end of the lesson, cut out the necessary shapes from tulle. The easy way to do this is to make a tracing of the shapes and place this over the tulle, then cut through the pattern and the tulle at the same time. Pin the tulle quite taut over a drawing of the shapes using long, glass-headed pins. A cake board is ideal for pressing pins into.

**1.** Pipe filigree over the tulle with yellow royal icing and a No1 tube. Edge all shapes with straight piped lines, and edge the curves with a tiny shell still using a No1 tube. Also make the semi-circle section, outline the shape with a No1 tube and flood in with yellow run-icing.

**2.** Secure the longest of the two straight pieces onto a curved former to dry, a ring of plastic rainwater piping is ideal.

**3.** When all the parts are dry, assemble them as shown, sticking together with royal icing. Small pieces of polystyrene may be required to support the sides until dry.

**4.** Make an arrangement of small sugar flowers and attach these inside the casket. You could use piped, royal-iced flowers as shown or cutter-type flowers made from paste. Attach two lids as shown, leaving a space between each. Edge the casket with a picot dot edging piped in yellow icing using a No0 tube.

## Mother's Day Cake

A delightful cake for Mother's Day.
Bake a shallow cake to give this modern
appearance. Coat the cake in cream-
coloured royal icing and edge with lilac-
coloured shells using a No44 tube.
Chocolate-coloured icing is used to
edge the shells on the cake top and to
pipe a filigree edge around the coated
base board. Position the filigree casket
on the cake top and pipe the inscription
using chocolate-coloured icing and a
No1 tube. A narrow cream-coloured
ribbon and bow complete the cake.

## Engagement Cake

Coat a cake in white royal icing and
edge with a shell border top and base
using a No44 tube. Edge the shells with
a fine rope using a No1 tube with lilac-
coloured icing from the top edge and
pink for the base. Pipe filigree to cover
the coated cake board using a No0 tube
and lilac-coloured icing. Use a strip of
greaseproof (waxed) paper marked off
in equal sections around the cake side.
Pipe a bulb of white icing at each
marker, remove the paper template.
Using a No1 tube and lilac icing, pipe
loops from each dot, allow to dry. Now
pipe a deeper loop from each dot, this
time using pink-coloured icing. Attach
the filigree ring casket and complete
the cake with a directly piped
inscription.

# Engagement Ring Casket

**1.** Prepare the runout sections of the casket using the templates provided. Outline in white using a No1 tube, flood with white run-icing, allow to dry.

**2.** Pipe small squares of filigree then place runout section over them, lining up with heart-shaped cutout section, repeat in all sections.

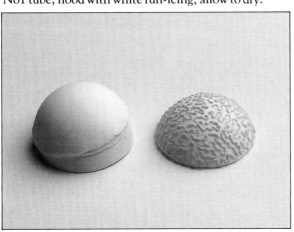

**3.** Roll out some sugarpaste or flower paste. Cover half a table tennis ball with paste, allow to dry, then pipe pink filigree all over dome using a No0 tube.

**4.** Assemble the runout sections as shown using small pieces of polystyrene to support until dry.

**5.** Pipe pink filigree over the assembled dry casket using a No0 tube. Roll out some pink sugarpaste approx. 10mm (½in) thick and cut out a disc as shown. Pipe a small bulb of icing into the base of the casket and position the sugarpaste disc. While the sugarpaste disc is still soft, insert a toy engagement ring at an angle as shown.

**6.** Attach the domed lid to the casket with royal icing and support with a small piece of foam sponge until set. Decorate the casket edges and the dome with a picot dot edging. A piped flower on the dome completes the casket.

# Filigree Cradle

**1.** Using the same method as described for the tulle casket, make the necessary pieces for the cradle as shown using the templates provided.

**2.** Shape the base of the cradle over a curved former. The picture shows a cardboard tube taped to a photographic slide box.

**3.** Assemble the sections of the cradle as shown, edging the filigree with a tiny pink-coloured icing shell. Line the inside of the cradle with cotton wool and place on a small ball of flesh-coloured marzipan or sugarpaste for the baby's head. Rest the filigree cover over the baby. A few bows can also be attached.

## Filigree Christening Cake

Collars can also be produced using the filigree or netting type method of piping. Here we see top and base collars used in conjunction with the filigree cradle. This gives the cake a very delicate appearance.

Using the templates provided trace out the designs and secure to a work board. Cover the design with waxed paper and pipe trellis or netting as shown. Start by piping the outline shape of the collar and then fill in with the netting. Edge the top collars with a picot dot edging as shown. Using the drawing provided, cut out a template to assist in piping the linework design.

# Filigree Wedding Cake

Make the trellis pieces first. Trace the drawing provided and secure to your work board. Cover the design with waxed paper and pipe the outline first using a No1 tube and white royal icing. Next pipe in the trellis and flower pattern. Overpipe the trellis and flower to strengthen the piece when attached to the cake, the flower is overpiped in orange-coloured icing with a darker centre bulb. You will need 24 pieces for the three tier cake, six for each tier and six for the top ornament. When the pieces are dry, turn them over and overpipe them in white icing. This makes them more stable and looks better when the piece is viewed from both sides.

**1.** Cut a length of drawing paper to fit around the coated cake, the paper strip should be the height of the cake side.

**2.** With paper strip flat, measure length of paper. Divide into six equal sections. Mark measured sections on each side of paper, then draw a line across.

**3.** Make a tracing of the linework shape from the appropriate drawing and repeat the design in each of the six sections.

**4.** Carefully cut the shapes to produce the template as shown. Secure to the cake with masking tape and commence piping the linework.

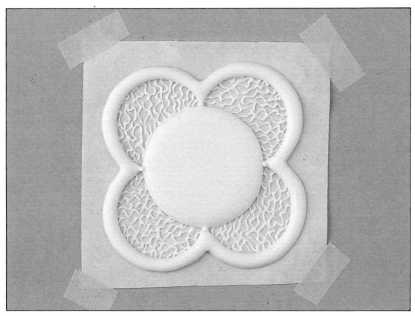

**5.** A runout disc is also required for the top ornament base.

**6.** Prepare templates from the drawings provided as shown and secure them to the cake with masking tape. Pipe lines on the cake top and side as shown using a No2 tube and white royal icing.

**7.** Remove the trellis pieces from the waxed paper and attach to the cake sides. A small silk, paste or piped flower and ribbon arrangement is attached to the cake with royal icing in each of the six side panels. For the cake top ornament, attach six trellis pieces together on a round runout disc, and insert a flower in each space between the pieces.

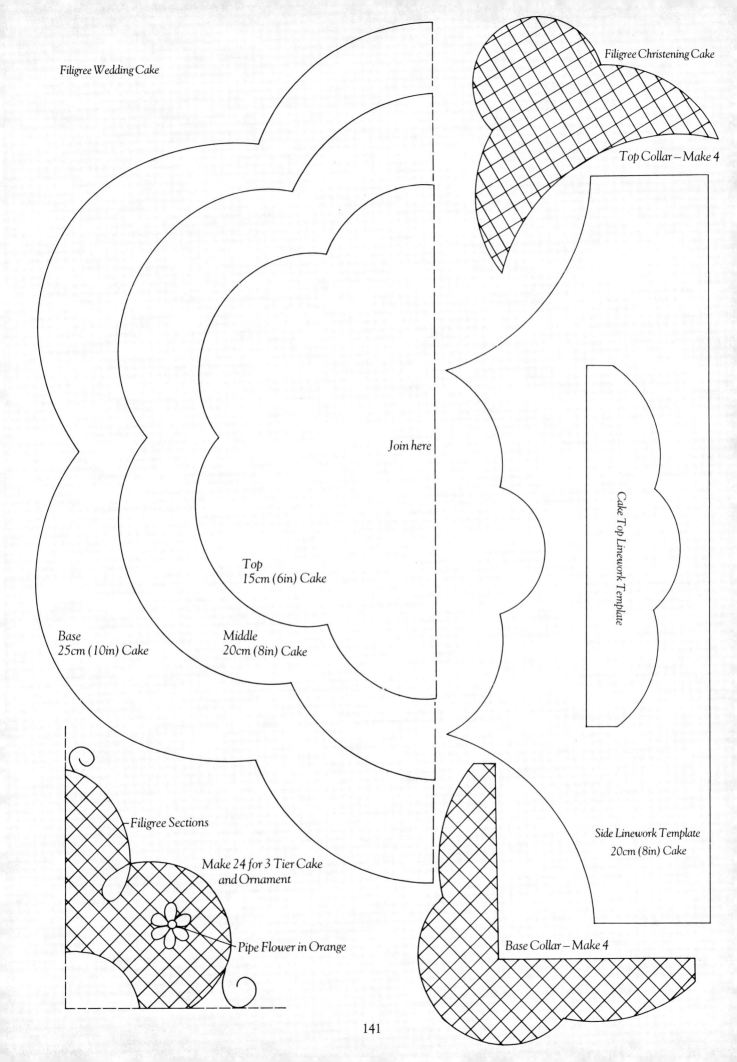

Filigree Wedding Cake

Filigree Christening Cake

Top Collar – Make 4

Join here

Cake Top Linework Template

Top
15cm (6in) Cake

Base
25cm (10in) Cake

Middle
20cm (8in) Cake

Filigree Sections

Make 24 for 3 Tier Cake
and Ornament

Pipe Flower in Orange

Side Linework Template
20cm (8in) Cake

Base Collar – Make 4

141

Base Tier Side Linework

Middle Tier Side Linework

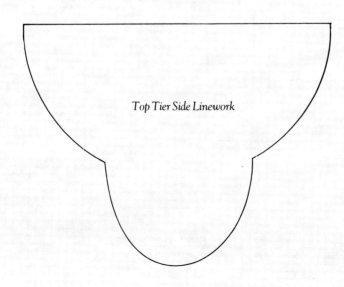

Top Tier Side Linework

*Filigree Wedding Cake*

Engagement Ring Casket

Top

Base

Sides – make 4

Filigree Cradle

Cradle – Curve over Former

This side straight

Curved side

Cradle Base

Cradle Canopy – Curve over Former

Canopy Insert – make 2

Cradle End

Diameter of curved former required

Mother's Day Casket

Filigree Lid – Make 2

Runout Base

Filigree Side Panel – Dry straight

Filigree Side – Dry curled over Former

Top

Middle

Base

# Advanced Figure Piping

# Advanced Figure Piping

**F**igure piping is one of the most frequently executed and certainly one of the most fascinating aspects of sugarcraft. Scope for the use of figure piping is endless, and is seen featured on cakes for every and any occasion.

Figure piping is particularly useful for original motif cakes, when few, if any of the available standard range of decorations are suitable. A figure to depict an occasion or celebration can more often than not be found and used as a centrepiece or as part of a scene or visual theme decoration. For years now, the art of figure piping has been used to adorn celebration cakes both commercially and by the enthusiastic competitor and exhibitor. Nearly every sugarcraft competition features classes with cakes requiring or being suitable to

incorporate a piped figure of some kind, particularly so in birthday and Christmas cake classes.

Every sugarcraft artist can use figure piping in their cake decoration, from the novice to the more experienced decorator. Each time you produce a figure you will no doubt become more experienced and adventurous, eventually making the most challenging and intricate designs and allowing your imagination to develop new and wonderful ideas for figures.

There are two main types of figure

piping – pressure-piped and freehand runout. The two styles may be used separately or they can be used together to good advantage; pressure-piped figure piping is probably not used as much nowadays, except commercially for simple, quick-to-pipe figures to give a hand-made appearance and personal finish to decorated cakes. The most popular freehand piped figures used today are the love birds seen on runout collars and on side panels of wedding cakes. Such work is also ideal for children's birthday cakes.

# Pressure-piped Figures

The technique for pressure-piped figure piping differs totally from that used for runout figure piping. Use fresh, well beaten royal icing, not too stiff but able to retain its shape when forced through the piping bag onto waxed paper or the surface medium of your coated cake. A fresh, light icing is preferred, as it will respond easily to the pressure put on it by your hand on the piping bag. This consistency of icing will produce bold shapes without the need for outlines, and can therefore be quickly built-up to form half-relief and full-relief figures. The main technique involved with free-hand figure piping is the amount of pressure used to control the flow of icing from the piping bag onto the waxed paper or cake surface. Three-quarters fill your piping bag with icing and neatly fold over the top of the bag to retain the contents and prevent seepage of the icing. The choice of piping tube will depend upon the size of the figure to be piped and the amount of fine detail required.

The following photographs and instructions show various figures piped in stages for you to follow. Once you have mastered these, it should be possible for you to develop other variations of your choice.

# Birds

**B**irds are a popular feature on wedding cakes. They are easy to make either in full- or half-relief.

## *Half-relief Birds*

**1.** Using a No1 tube, pipe left and right wings onto waxed paper as shown. Use a side-to-side movement when piping to build up the required shape. A couple of pencil lines drawn on paper beneath the waxed paper will help to achieve a consistent size. Allow the piped wings to dry.

**2.** Build up the body of the bird. This can be done directly on the cake surface or the birds can be piped onto waxed paper and allowed to dry before using as required. Pipe the wing first, using the same method as described previously. Next pipe a bulbous body using a No2 tube, taper the bulb as shown. Pipe on the tail feathers using a No1 tube. Now pipe a bulb for the head, then add a beak using a No1 tube. Finally insert a prepared, dry wing into the still soft body and position as required. Using the same method, but reversing the shapes, you can produce birds facing each other.

147

# Stork

The stork is an ideal motif to make for birth or christening cakes. The bow-tie colours are used to reflect the sex of the baby.

The stork is piped in much the same manner described for the swan, using a No3 tube for the neck and body. The wings are piped using a No2 tube. Pipe the beak with orange-coloured icing using a No1 tube and the legs in a coffee-orange colour again using a No1 tube. A bow-tie may be piped on waxed paper and attached to the stork. The template provided will make piping the stork easier for you – simply trace into position on the cake surface or plaque. When proficient, the template will not be required.

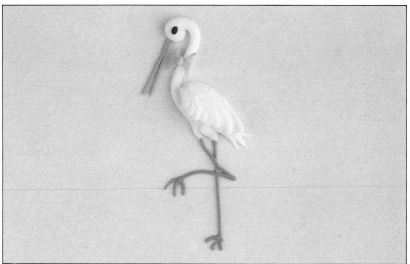

The stork is a favourite motif for christening cakes.

Here the stork motif is presented on a sugarpaste plaque edged with royal icing, useful as a prepared decoration for the top or if made smaller, for the sides of cakes.

# Duck Birthday Cake

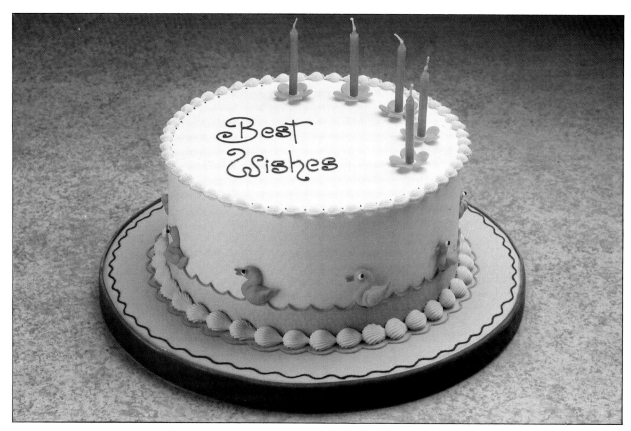

Here we see figure piping put to use as part of the decoration of a royal iced cake. The cake is coated in cream-coloured icing, and dried. Make a scalloped template from cartridge paper and position as shown on the cake side, secure the template with masking tape. Apply blue-coloured royal icing to the cake side exposed below the template and coat smooth using a palette knife or side scraper. Remove the template and coat the cake board with the same coloured icing. Pipe shell borders in cream-coloured icing using tube No 44. Edge the scalloped water frieze and the shell borders with blue icing. Using a No1 tube and chocolate-coloured icing, pipe dots on the top border shells, a wavy line on the cake board and the inscription. Attach prepared piped ducks to the cake side with royal icing. The candle holders are made by cutting sugarpaste with a petal cutter and forming in curved fruit trays or clean polystyrene egg boxes. Allow the holders to dry then attach them to the cake and position a candle in each.

# Duck

Use an orange-yellow icing and a No2 tube and pipe the head, neck and front of the body in one operation, using various pressures on the piping bag to create the required shape. Next pipe a pear-shaped body as shown. Pipe the same shape again, smaller to form the wing.

Finally pipe on the beak with bright orange icing. A chocolate or black eye completes the duck.

149

# Runout Figure Piping

**T**his second form of figure piping is used extensively nowadays by almost every sugarcraft artist. It is frequently seen in several classes of competitive sugarcraft, and can be suited to any occasion providing plenty of scope for new and original ideas.

Runout piped figures are normally produced on waxed paper to be peeled off when dry, the figure is then placed directly onto the prepared cake surface or onto an icing or sugarpaste plaque. This does not mean that every figure has to be made flat. Figures can also be made to take the curved shape of a round cake side, by producing and drying the runout on a curved former of the same diameter (or curve) as the cake on which it is to be attached.

A few things need to be considered before actual production of the figure can commence.

### Selection of Motif
Suitable figures and animals for possible use as runouts can be found in most children's annuals, on greeting cards and on gift-wrapping paper. Before such figures could be used commercially, full permission would have to be obtained from the copyright owner. If on the other hand you prefer to be more creative, you could use various ideas and put them together to create your own original figure or motif. The main point to remember at this stage is to choose a figure that you can execute reasonably well, do not select a really intricate design if your piping and runout skills are limited. It is far better to choose a simpler figure that you know will be easy to reproduce.

### The Correct Figure Size
Having selected the figure or animal of your choice the next stage is to ensure that it will comfortably fit in the space allocated for it on your cake. Sometimes you may have figures that you have used previously for another cake and wish to reduce or enlarge for further use. Or it may be that you have seen a figure you want to use but it does not fit on your cake. See lesson 9 (page 109) for details on methods of enlarging and reducing designs.

An alternative method to those already suggested would be to invest in a pantograph. This implement is usually plastic and consists of a painter which is used to follow the outline of the original drawing, while on the other end a pencil transfers the reduced or enlarged image. Again this may not be economically practical, the investment will obviously depend on the amount of design work you intend to undertake.

### Interpreting Designs
The basic idea of a runout figure is that an outline is piped and the various sections of the figure separated. Into each section, run-icing is piped either in white, to be painted when dry, or in appropriate colours, again which can be painted with further detail. The figures may vary in one of four ways, according to the filling in and finishing techniques.

**The types of figure piping are: semi-relief, outline, wafer-thin and full-relief**

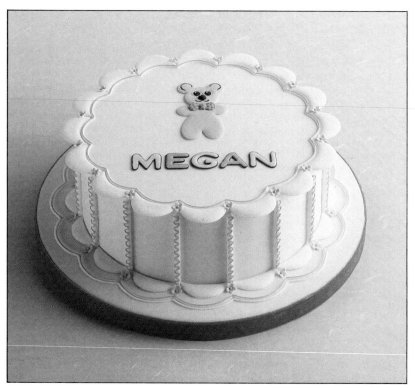

## Teddy Christening Cake

The pink semi-relief teddy is used here as an attractive figure decoration for this royal iced cake. First make several runout sections for the borders. Using the template provided, outline in white royal icing using a No1 tube and then flood in with white run-icing. The side design is made by piping lines of white royal icing onto waxed paper, the same length as the depth of the cake side. When the lines are dry, a pink wavy line is piped on using a No1 tube. Attach the prepared lines to the side of a pink coated cake. Next attach the prepared runout sections to the top edge and base board. Attach small blossom flowers, made with a cutter and piped with a tiny centre bulb. Pipe linework around the inside edge of the top runout sections, and to follow the base border. Runout lettering completes the cake.

# Semi-relief

This type of figure piping is the simplest form that includes flood work, it is basically an outline with sections, flooded in and allowed to dry. For all runout figure work you need to start with a tracing of your design, copied onto cartridge paper and then placed flat on your surface. Cover the design with a suitably sized piece of waxed paper and secure it to the board with masking tape.

In the first example shown the rabbit figure is outlined in a deep orange-colour and flooded with a lighter orange run-icing. The eyes are flooded in with white run-icing. When dry, paint on the mouth and ear detail with brown food colouring and a fine paintbrush. The nose and buttons are piped on with coloured royal icing.

The pink teddy bear figure is produced in the same way with a separate runout bow-tie attached to the dried figure.

# Outline Figures

A simple but very effective way of introducing figures onto your cakes. Outline figures are piped directly onto the cake surface of royal icing, sugarpaste or fondant. Trace the figure required onto the prepared cake surface, use the jolly Jack-in-the-box figure to experiment with. Prepare piping bags of royal icing in the required colours all with a No1, 0 or 00 tubes depending upon the fineness or detail involved. Using the prepared tubes, pipe the outlines of the figures in each of the appropriate colours.

## Wafer Thin

This is a very modern method of figure piping which is now very popular. The aim is to achieve a really thin runout figure, the thinness being determined by the tube being used, in most cases a No1 tube.

Prepare the drawing and cover with waxed paper as before. Outline the design with brown royal icing using a No1 tube, use a compound colour to achieve a rich brown without diluting the icing consistency. Allow the outline to dry a little and then flood in each area with the appropriate colour of run-icing. Extra detail can be painted on when the figure is dry if required.

## Full-relief

Full-relief figure piping is started in the same manner as semi-relief piping, by outlining a shape on waxed paper. With this method, however, each section is piped in a different manner to achieve a more detailed figure with definite modelling and roundness to parts of the figure. Some parts, such as those farthest away, for instance, the main part of the body on the teddy, are flooded in flat. The arms, legs and ears are flooded in a more bulbous fashion to produce the necessary roundness. As a basic rule for flooding procedure, flood in the parts that appear farthest away, then build up the flood work, allowing sections to dry before flooding adjacent sections. The final parts of the flood work should be those that appear nearest to you.

A simple method to make the flood work sequence easier is to number the parts of the body on the drawings before flooding as shown. In this way you can then flood all parts marked '1', allow them to dry then flood parts marked '2' and so on until the figure is completed.

Full-relief figure piping sequence for teddy bear motif, using one colour of icing only.

## Combination Work

If you runout the figure in a single colour of icing as for the teddy bear, you can paint on extra fine detail and shading once the figure has dried, using edible food colours with a fine paintbrush. Here we see a finish sometimes referred to as built-up figure piping. This is the use of extra runout or piped sections added to a basic figure to form a built-up motif, for instance, the runout ribbon and bow and the piped flower and stem.

## Teddy Birthday Cake

An attractive hexagonal-shaped cake decorated with pale blue and white royal icing. The runout collars are made using the template provided, outlining in a No1 tube. The board linework is piped using a card template prepared from the collar design. Complete the cake with a runout teddy figure and directly piped inscription.

153

# Flower Girl

This very attractive little figure is useful for many occasional cakes. The figure is based on full-relief figure piping, this time flooding in with appropriately coloured run-icing. These types of figures can be runout onto waxed paper and completed before attaching to the cake. When you become more proficient at figure piping you could execute the work directly onto the royal iced or sugarpaste surface.

Notice how the build-up of the dress has been completed in stages, to allow individual sections to dry before flooding adjacent sections.

The finished figure painted with edible food colouring and built-up in the form of a bunch of piped flowers and stems.

*Rabbit Low-Relief Figure*

*Teddy Low-Relief Figure*

*Top Border Runout Pieces for Pink Christening Cake*

*Base Border Runout Pieces*

*Jack in the box*

*Girl Figure*

*Flooding Sequence For Full-Relief Piping*

*Santa Wafer Thin Figure*

*Stork*

*Bow Tie*

*Swan*

*Duck Birthday Cake*

*Water Wave Template secured to cake side ready*

*for application of blue icing.*

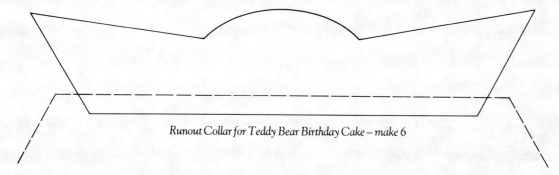

*Runout Collar for Teddy Bear Birthday Cake – make 6*

# Advanced Runout Work and Freestanding Runouts

# Crown Ornament

*Having now mastered basic and intermediate runout work, and gained an understanding of the characteristics and possibilities of this work, more advanced runout work may now be tackled.*

**1.** Using the drawings provided, trace them onto cartridge paper and secure to your work-board. Outline using a No1 tube and white icing and flood with white run-icing. Make six runout pieces and allow to dry. Using the same template again, place waxed paper over and pipe a scalloped net filigree pattern as shown using a No1 tube, outline the work with the same tube and immediately place a prepared runout section onto the net work and gently press to attach the two together. Repeat on all six sections and allow to dry. Also make a runout hexagon shape using the drawing provided, this will form the base of the crown.

**2.** For the points of the crown, cut out shapes from tulle. Trace the drawing provided onto paper and place onto six thicknesses of tulle, cut through the template and the tulle at the same time. Using a drawing of the full template, place a piece of waxed paper over and secure with masking tape. Secure a tulle shape with a few dots of royal icing, then continue as for conventional runout work. Outline in white using a No1 tube and flood in with white run-icing.

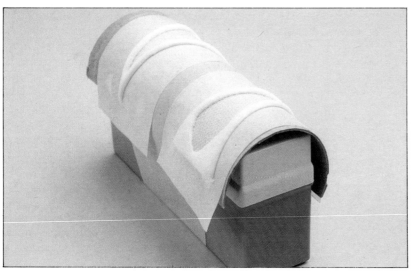

**3.** Place the shapes onto curved formers made from cardboard tubes as shown. Allow the runout shapes to dry, then pipe a tiny shell edging on the inside edge near the tulle.

**4.** Assemble the six side runout sections and base as shown, attach with royal icing. Use small blocks of polystyrene to support the pieces until fully dry.

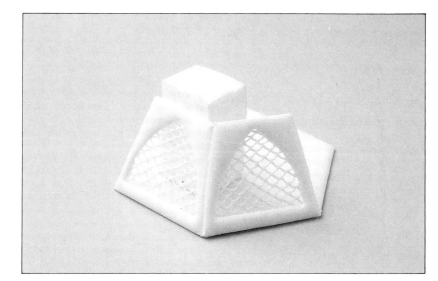

**5.** Once the base formation is dry, the points of the crown can be attached, again using royal icing. Blocks of polystyrene each of the same height are used to support the points until dry. Pipe a tiny shell using a No1 tube as shown around the joins and edges.

**6.** An arrangement of artificial, silk, paste or piped flowers is then placed inside the crown, the crown is then positioned and attached on the wedding cake top as required.

# Double Collars

**D**ouble collars provide an interesting and refreshing change to the conventional single collar. Ensure your drawing and piping is accurate for double collar work, as any inaccuracies are exaggerated.

Use the drawing provided to try a double collar. Your own designs can easily be adapted to make double collars, by drawing in a second outline, a small distance from the original outline. To emphasise the double collar, outline and flood in the under collar with a slightly darker colour than that of the top collar.

## Pink Celebration Cake

A very detailed cake top design requiring the use of double base boards to balance the overall effect. Note the double collars with filigree overlays.

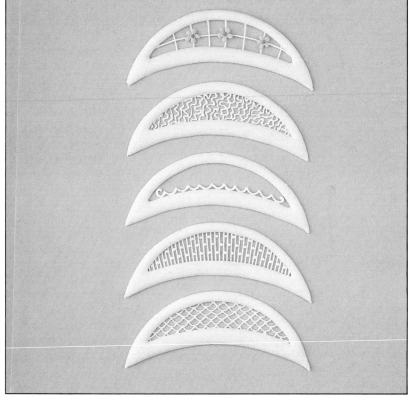

## Runout Collar Fillers

The photograph shows five variations on the basic collar section used on the Pink Celebration Cake. This is another example of creative sugarcraft, making one basic idea work for you with several options on decorative finishes. The templates are at the end of the lesson.

**1.** Piped criss-cross lines decorated with a piped flower.

**2.** Piped filigree using a No0 or No1 tube.

**3.** Scallop edging piped using a No1 tube then overpiped.

**4.** Line and dot. Using a No1 tube pipe the lines first and then pipe in the dots.

**5.** Scalloped net filigree piped using a No1 tube.

# Runout Church

The runout church is ideal for a Christmas cake decoration or made in white icing and left unpainted would make an unusual ornament for a winter wedding.

**1.** Make templates for all the sections of the church, then outline and flood in all shapes to make runout pieces. Notice how the clock face is flooded with icing to make painting detail easier.

**2.** When the runout pieces are dry, attach pieces of tulle cut to size on the back of each window. For stained glass windows the tulle can be painted with food colouring.

**3.** Using edible food colouring, paint the brickwork detail on all the church walls and the two visible roof sections. Outline the window frames with brown royal icing and a No0 tube.

**4.** Assemble the church, using royal icing and supporting the sections with polystyrene blocks until dry.

**5.** Prepare a sugarpaste plaque in an oval shape. A fluted edge looks attractive as shown, use a large oval food cutter or make a template from card. Brush the plaque with softened royal icing, leaving a section clear for the inscription.

Model a few small trees from green marzipan. Make cone shapes from the marzipan and snip them with small scissors to make branches. Brush with icing to represent snow.

Attach the church and brush a little softened icing on to represent snow. While the icing is still soft sprinkle with granulated sugar to give a frosty effect.

# Anniversary Cake Ornament

**1.** Make two runout shapes as shown, using the drawings provided.

**2.** Make the runout numerals. Outline the numerals with white royal icing, allow to dry. Paint the outlines with silver food colour. Flood in the numerals with white runicing. This technique creates attractive figures with silver edges and white centres.

Assemble the ornament using the floating collar technique.

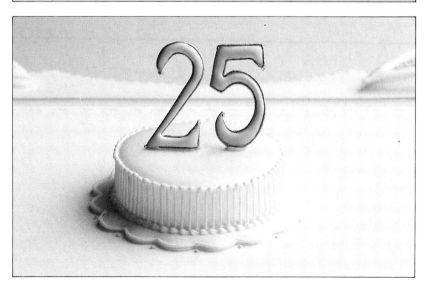

**3.** Floating Collar Anniversary Ornament.

# Floating Collar Anniversary Cake

**1.** Make the top and base collar using the drawings provided. Coat the cake in white royal icing. The cake is presented on a double cake board. Coat the cake and board in the conventional manner, then attach the cake and board to a second board 2.5cm (1in) larger than the first board. Fill the space between the boards and smooth flat at an angle from the board to the other using a side scraper or palette knife.

**2.** Make four runout overlays and then pipe blue filigree onto waxed paper as shown. Place the dry runout section over the filigree and attach with a gentle pressure.

**3.** Place about eight wooden blocks of even size (smooth edges and corners with sandpaper to ensure easy release of blocks) around the cake board then place the base collar over the cake and rest on the blocks. Pipe a line using a No1 tube on the cake board directly beneath the collar edge, follow the shape exactly. This can be done before placing the base collar on, using a template as a guide. Now pipe lines from the base board up to the collar edge as shown at regular intervals, use a No1 or No0 tube. Pipe at intervals around the base, allow these first lines to take the weight of the runout collar. The blocks can then be removed and line piping completed.

This stunning 25th Anniversary cake uses many sugarcraft techniques, the main feature being the floating collars.

**4.** Using a ruler resting along the cake side, scratch a straight line onto the cake side using a No1 tube. Pipe a straight line along the inside edge of the base collar. Allow these lines to dry, then pipe lines from the side line down onto the collar as shown, again at regular intervals using a No1 or No0 tube. Finish with a tiny piped shell along the straight lines. Attach the top collar.

**5.** Using prepared blocks of wood, shaped at an angle, place a block on each corner of the top collar. Then position the prepared shield shaped runout overlay pieces on the wooden blocks. Again pipe a few lines on each side to support the overlay, then remove the blocks and continue the line piping.

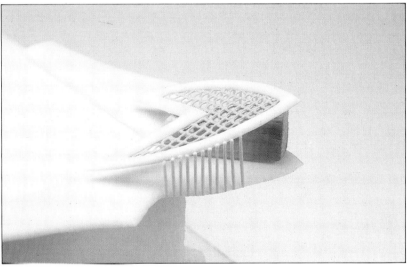

**6.** Pipe a tiny picot dot edging around the edge of the top collar. Then pipe 3,2,1, linework around the inside edge of the top collar and following the outside edge of the base linework shape. An arrangement of ribbons, bows and flowers at each corner completes the cake.

Base

Tower Side    Tower Front

Back

Front

Side

Roof

Tower Roof    Doors    Porch

Template for Runout Church

Pink Celebration Cake

Overlay – Make 4

Under collar darker pink

Centrepiece Top

Trellis and Flower

Scallop Line

Line and Dot

Scalloped Net Filigree

Centrepiece Top

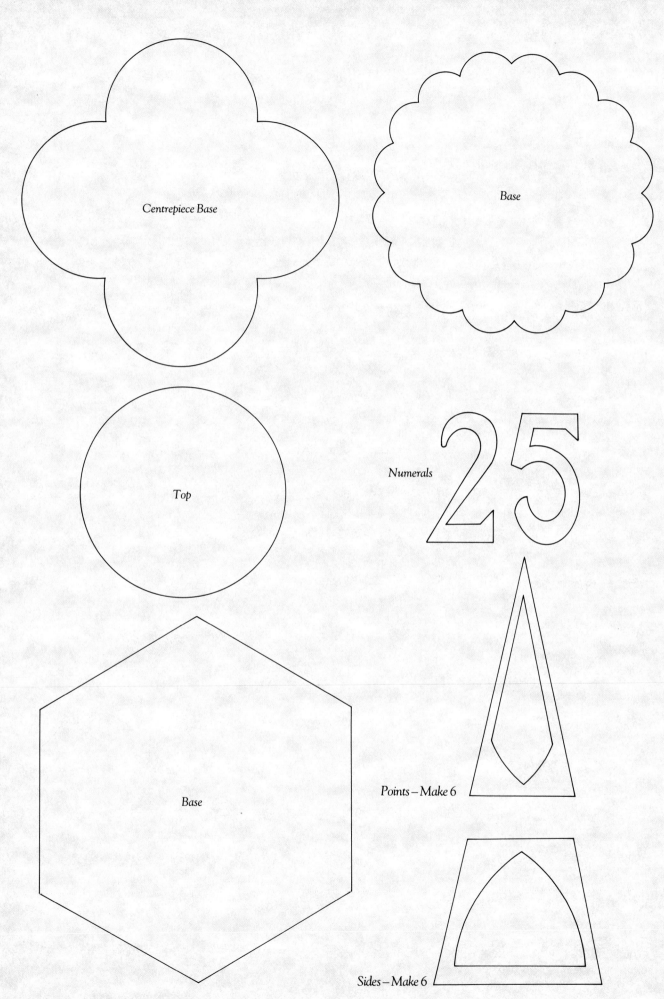

Centrepiece Base

Base

Top

Numerals

Base

Points – Make 6

Sides – Make 6

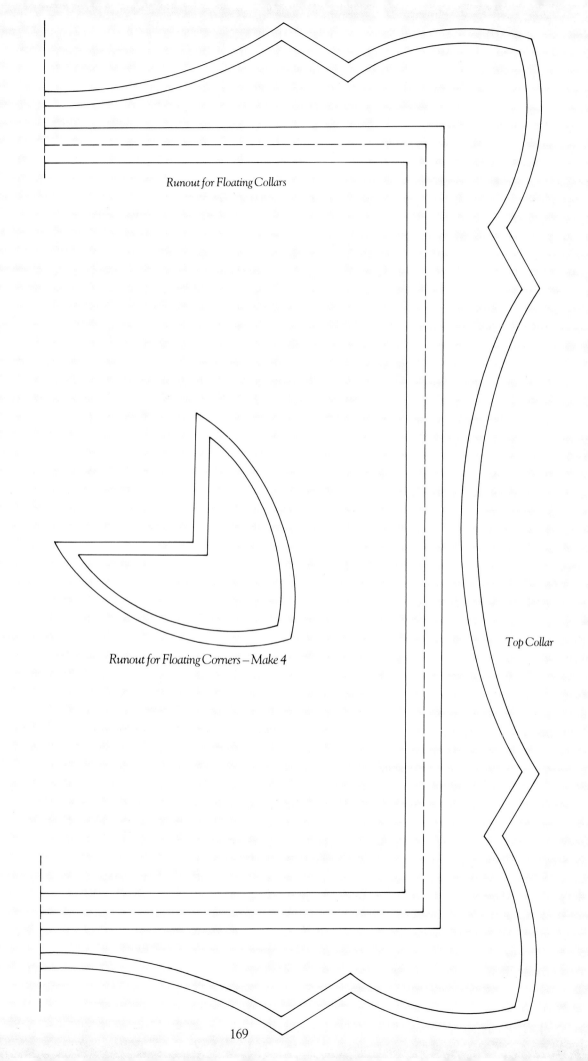

*Runout for Floating Collars*

*Runout for Floating Corners – Make 4*

*Top Collar*

*Make one in white for Wedding Bell
or in green for Festive Bell*

*Templates for Festive Bell and Wedding Bells Ornament*

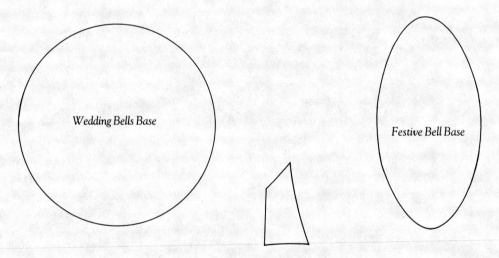

*Wedding Bells Base*

*Festive Bell Base*

*Runout Support for Festive Bell*

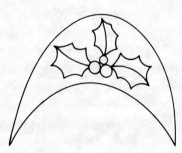

*Holly Insert for Festive Bell*

*Runout Christmas Scene – Paint when dry*

170

# Introduction to Sugar Flowers

# Equipment

### Equipment
The equipment used for making sugar flowers is quite specialized and is in addition to the basic cake decorating equipment. A sewing, fishing or craft box is ideal for storing this equipment as you will collect a great number of small items such as stamens and cutters which are best kept together.

### Anger tool
Use for opening the throats of flowers.

### Confectioner's glaze
This is a special liquid which gives a shine to leaves and flowers.

### Cutters
There is a vast selection of petal and leaf cutters available.

### Dresden pewter tool
This is useful for creating special effects, such as getting the right tilt to the large petal of a pansy.

### Floral tape
Use this for covering wires and for assembling sprays.

### Foam rubber
Many decorators work over a large square of thick foam rubber so that if a flower gets dropped it does not shatter. Smaller pieces of foam are needed for ejecting cutter flowers, for lifting and shaping petals and for protection while transporting finished sprays.

### Glass-headed pins
These have a variety of uses in cake decorating. In flower modelling, they can be used like ball tools for small petals.

### Leaf formers
Rubber veiners designed for the pottery industry make realistic sugar leaves.

### Pliers
Use small long-nosed pliers for bending wire and electrical pliers for stripping wire.

### Polystyrene block
Use this for holding the flowers before they are wired into sprays.

### Ribbed tool
Use for finger flowers.

### Ribbons
All sugar flower sprays contain ribbons. Very narrow ones are best for this, and for ribbon insertion and banding. Wider ribbons can be used to cover cake boards.

### Stamens
These come in many different shapes, sizes and colours.

### Tape shredder
This is useful for cutting the floral tape into narrow strips.

### Tweezers
Fine-pointed crank-ended craft tweezers are best for delicate work.

### Wire cutters
Use for cutting the florists' wire, or keep a pair of floristry scissors specially for the job.

### Wires
A selection of covered florist wire in different gauges is needed. Use fine wire for small flowers and heavier gauge for large flowers. Fine rose wire or fuse wire is useful for wiring together sprays.

# Flower Paste

All of the moulded flowers in this book have been made using this recipe for flower paste. However, there are many variations on this recipe, so experiment to find one which suits you. Remember that flower paste is affected by climate, and if you live in a very humid place, then you may need to add more cornflour (cornstarch) and reduce the amount of icing sugar.

425g (14oz/3½ cups) icing (confectioner's) sugar, sifted
60g (2oz/¼ cup) cornflour (cornstarch)
15ml (3 teaspoons) gum tragacanth
or
10ml (2 teaspoons) gum tragacanth and 10ml (2 teaspoons) carboxy methyl cellulose
25ml (5 teaspoons) cold water
10ml (2 teaspoons) powdered gelatine
15ml (3 teaspoons) white fat (shortening)
10ml (2 teaspoons) liquid glucose
white of one large egg, string removed

Sift together the sugar and cornflour (cornstarch) in the bowl of a heavy-duty mixer. Sprinkle over the gum tragacanth, or the gum tragacanth and carboxy methyl cellulose. Place the mixer bowl over a large pan of boiling water. Cover the top with a dry cloth, and then with a plate or cake board.

Put the water in a small glass bowl and sprinkle the powdered gelatine over it. Leave to sponge.

Half fill a small saucepan with water and place over a low heat. Bring to just below the boiling point. Place the bowl of sponged gelatine over the pan and stir in the liquid glucose and the white fat. Stir until the fat is melted.

When the icing sugar feels warm, take the bowl off the pan of boiling water, dry the bottom and place on the mixer. Remove the beater from the other pan, dry and assemble the mixer. Add the gelatine solution and the egg white to the sugar. Cover the bowl with a cloth, and turn the mixer to the slowest speed. Mix until all the ingredients are combined and the paste is a dull beige colour.

Turn the mixer to maximum and beat until the paste is white and stringy. This will take 5-10 minutes. Remove the paste from the bowl and place in a clean plastic bag. Place the bag in an airtight container and refrigerate for at least 24 hours before using. If planning to store the paste for a few weeks, put it in four or five small bags and open one at a time.

To use the paste, cut off a small piece, add a smear of white fat and dip into some egg white before working. The warmth of your hands will bring the paste to a workable, elastic consistency. Remember that the paste dries out very quickly, so keep it covered at all times and never cut off more than a very small piece. Certain colours, particularly reds and violets, may change the consistency, so it may be necessary to add more white fat and egg white.

## Quick Flower Paste

This paste is easier to make, but the flowers will not be as delicate.
225g (8oz) commercial sugarpaste
5ml (1 teaspoon) gum tragacanth
white fat (shortening)
Knead the sugarpaste and gum tragacanth together, adding a small amount of white fat to get an elastic consistency. Store and use as for the previous recipe.

## Hints and Tips

Flower paste and modelling paste are affected by the warmth of your hands. A cake decorator with very warm hands would need to use a slightly firmer paste than someone with cold hands.

Always colour pastes with paste food colourings, not liquid ones, which will change the consistency of the modelling pastes. Add the colour using the end of a cocktail stick.

After colouring flower paste or sugarpaste, put it in a plastic bag and return it to the refrigerator for a few minutes. Kneading in the colour will make the paste warm and stringy, and it will be difficult to work with.

Many colours, particularly yellows and reds, will deepen on standing, so colour the paste a shade lighter than the desired finished colour.

An alternative method of colouring flowers is to make them all white, cream or a pale shade then petal dust to the desired shade when dry.

Petal dust is a powdered food colouring based on cornflour (cornstarch), which can be mixed in with the petal dust in small quantities to obtain a lighter shade.

Flower paste should be rolled as thinly as possible so that the petals will be translucent and natural looking. Paste can be rolled out on a thin film of white fat (shortening) or on a light dusting of cornflour (cornstarch). Experiment to find which one works best for you.

When doing double frilling as in an orchid throat or carnation, the paste should be slightly thicker than usual or it will not frill successfully.

If using cornflour (cornstarch) to dust the work surface, place it in a square of butter muslin (cheesecloth) tied in a bag, or use a pepper pot for a miniature flour dredger.

# Making Sugar Flowers

Take a small piece of paste, colour it if required with paste food colouring, work a little white vegetable fat and egg white into the paste until it is elastic and pliable, and work until the paste is warm as cold paste is extremely difficult to shape. Roll out the paste using a special small board and pin. Sprinkle the board with a light coating of cornflour (cornstarch) to prevent the paste from sticking, but avoid using excessive amounts or the paste will dry out and crack.

**1.** Start rolling the paste on a light dusting of cornflour (cornstarch). Check that it is translucent, if you cannot see through the paste it is too thick and requires further rolling.

**2.** Place your cutter on the surface of the paste and with your fingers evenly over the cutter press down to cut out the shape.

**3.** To soften petals for flowers such as a sweet pea, use a cocktail stick and gently roll over the edge of the petal in a gentle motion. This is a very different principle from frilling as for the carnation.

**4.** Cup the petals on a piece of soft, sponge rubber using a dog bone or ball tool. The more pressure you apply the more cupped the petal will become.

**5.** Petals and foliage will sometimes have to be veined. The tool shown is made specially for this purpose but a cocktail stick or porcupine quill could be used instead. As with cupping, veining has to be done on sponge. Do not put too much pressure on the petal or tool, but use a gentle stroking movement along the length of the petal or leaf.

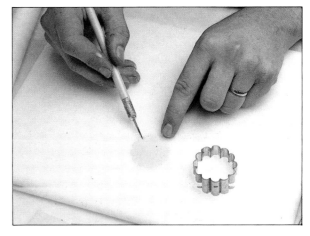

**6.** On most flowers, especially pulled flowers, cutting plays an important part in the shape of the flower. Although a small kitchen knife can be used, better results will be achieved with a modelling or craft knife. For instance, small cuts put along the edge of the carnation petal prior to frilling.

**7.** Many flowers have to be frilled. Use a wooden cocktail stick and frill the outer edges of the petal with a firm rolling movement in a back and forward direction, take care to keep the paste moving all the time to ensure that it does not stick.

**8.** Stick petals and attach to each other with fresh egg white using a small clean paintbrush, but do not leave this in the egg white when it is not needed or you will apply too much to the surface of the paste. The petal here is being brushed with egg white prior to folding onto the wire of the carnation.

# Making Foliage or Individually Wired Petals

**1.** Take a piece of paste, squash between your thumb and first finger and, using a paintbrush, handle as a miniature rolling-pin. Start rolling the paste retaining a thick part at the end nearest to you. Then roll from the left and right hand sides in order to thin the paste evenly all the way over, but leaving it thicker at one end.

**2.** Cut out the leaf or petal. The base of the cutter should be over the thicker part of the paste.

**3.** Take a piece of 28- to 30-gauge green covered wire in your right hand, dip the hooked end in a little egg white, then pick up the leaf holding firmly between the thumb and first finger of your left hand. Push the wire into the leaf, the pressure ensures that the wire goes in straight and stops it from piercing through the paste. The wire needs to go in about 6mm (¼in).

**4.** Take the leaf and place on a rubber or plastic veiner. Then place on a piece of sponge rubber and, using a veining tool, mark the central vein to give the leaf more character. Vein on both sides.

# Colouring Flowers

**1.** For certain flowers you will need a greater density of colour than dusting alone can give, for these you need to paint the petals. Mix a little petal dust or paste colour with some clear spirit (gin or vodka). Spirit is used for this purpose as it evaporates and dries quickly and does not soften the paste. However, mix only small quantities of colour as it too will evaporate while you work. Here the dots are being painted on the throat of a foxglove using a plum colour and a No00 paintbrush.

**2.** To get a soft overall effect on your sugar flowers you will need a soft round No4 brush. Here a honeysuckle flower is dusted a creamy-yellow shade; note how the plate is used like an artist's palette to mix the colours.

**3.** If a stronger density of colour is required on the outer edge of the petal only, a short, firm, flat brush should be used. Work with a gentle stroking movement from the outside of the petal to the inside. Using this principle, the spray carnation can have a contrasting colour on the petal edges.

**4.** Here a blackberry leaf is dusted prior to varnishing, again a flat, firm brush has to be used. The copper colour is used to give a little depth to the leaf and is brushed down one side of the leaf only.

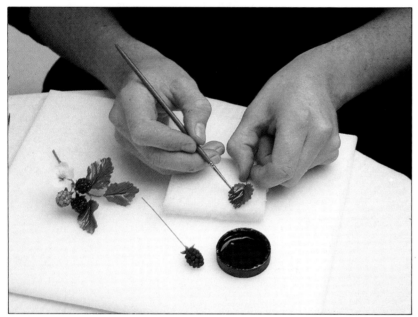

**5.** There are several ways to achieve a shiny surface on foliage. The method used here employs a commercially available confectioner's glaze used in the bakery for varnishing marzipan and chocolate for display purposes. It is edible but has an unpleasant taste. Brush the glaze over the surface of the foliage and stick the wire in a stand for about 15 minutes to dry. Two other methods you can use for shining the surface of the paste are painting with gum arabic glaze, or the leaves may be held in the steam of a kettle for a few seconds. This gives a gloss finish but it is prone to going matt in damp or humid weather.

**6.** Here confectioner's glaze is being used on blackberry fruits. Once you have finished using your brush, clean in a spirit based cleaner, such as white spirit or dry cleaning fluid.

# Daffodil Leaf

Leaves may be made very quickly and effectively using floristry tape. This tape is available in a variety of shades and may be coloured with dust.

**1.** Cut a piece of wire approximately the length of the leaf you want, and a slightly longer piece of floristry tape.

**2.** Take the floristry tape and stretch it, this opens up the tape releasing a glue so it sticks to itself.

**3.** Place the tape on the work surface, lay the wire on to it and then bring the long end back on itself over the top of the wire.

**4.** Now run your finger over the surface of the leaf to stick the two sides together.

**5.** Take a pair of small sharp scissors and cut out the leaf shape. This is a daffodil so it is a long, thin leaf with a pointed end.

**6.** The finished daffodil leaf with its two cut sides.

**7.** Here is a mimosa leaf made in the same way, but it has a more regular leaf shape. Take a pair of sharp scissors and make cuts at an angle up the leaf.

**8.** Continue until you have cut both sides and achieved a feathered effect.

**9.** Twist the leaf in a spiral to give a 3-dimensional effect.

**10.** Here the finished two leaves and a finished spray of mimosa.

# Pulled Flowers

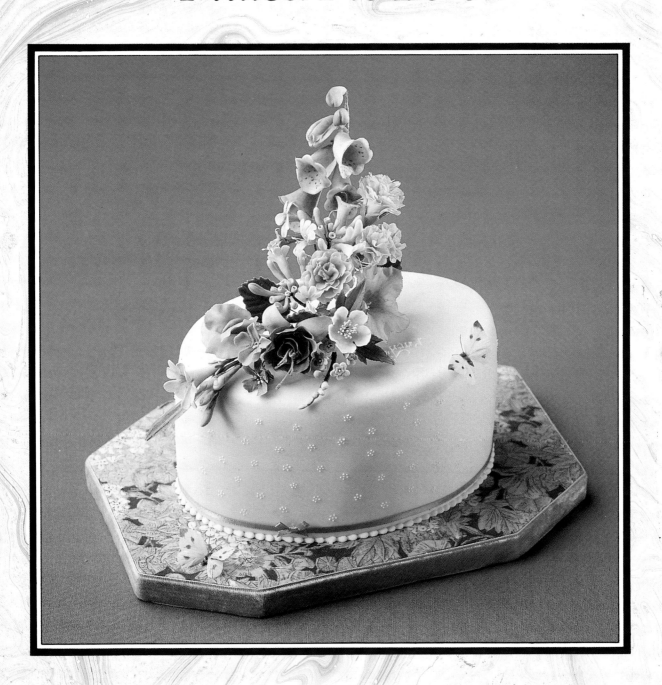

# Pulled and Finger Flowers

**H**and-moulded flowers are usually known as pulled or finger flowers. They are the easiest flowers to start with as little special equipment is needed.

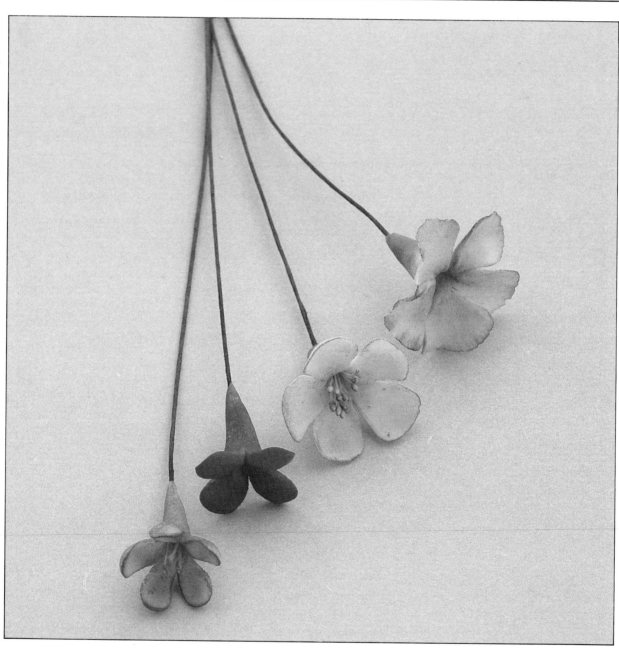

This lesson begins with pulled basic blossom which is the easiest flower to master and progresses to more complicated flowers like the snowdrop. The more difficult flowers are featured towards the end of the chapter so if you have never made any pulled flowers before, it is best to begin with those at the beginning of the chapter. Remember that the smaller the piece of paste that you begin with, the smaller the finished flower and the more fiddly it is to perfect. It is better to start off with a larger piece of paste, perfect the flower, then reduce down the size rather than risk becoming frustrated and disappointed working with tiny petals. Making evenly shaped petals and perfectly balanced flowers comes with practice, and the more practice you have the better your finished flowers will be.

| EQUIPMENT |
| --- |
| Sharp modelling knife |
| Wooden modelling stick |
| Dowel or end of paintbrush |
| Modelling tools |
| Petal dust |
| Paste food colouring |
| Wire |
| Floristry tape |
| Stamens |

# Basic Blossom

**1.** Take a pea-sized piece of flower-paste, this should be thoroughly kneaded so that it is soft and warm.

**2.** Mould into a small cone shape, dip the pointed end of your dowel into cornflour (cornstarch) and insert into the thick end of the cone.

**3.** Taking a sharp modelling knife make five equal sized cuts for the five petals. The cuts should be one-quarter to one-third of the total length of the cone.

**4.** Remove the dowel and open up the flower by pushing your finger into the centre.

**5.** Taking each petal in turn process by squashing, pinching and pulling.

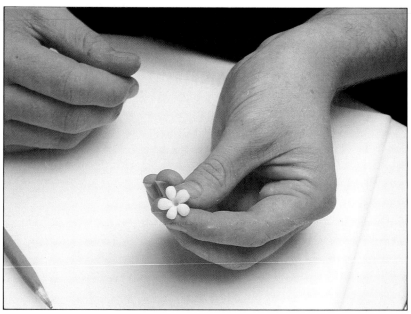

**6.** You should end up with a flower with five equal petals, but remember this will only be perfected with practice.

**7.** Place your wooden stick back into the throat of the flower and pull the petals up slightly to produce a nice shaped flower. Remove the stick.

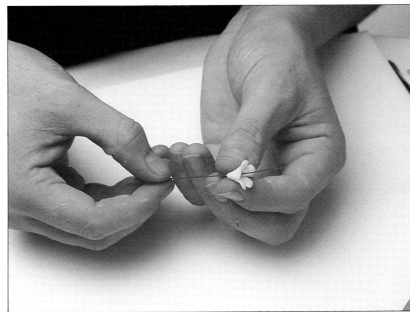

**8.** Take a piece of 28 or 30-gauge covered wire. The wire usually comes in packs with long strands, cut each one into four to give lengths of wire suitable for most flowers and sufficient to wire the flowers into sprays without being wasteful. Bend the wire to make a small hook on one end, dip the hooked end into a little fresh egg white and thread through the throat of the flower, as shown.

**9.** Pull the wire through until it sits into the soft paste at the back of the flower. Squash the flower back around the wire. You now have a finished blossom on wire.

# Winter Jasmine

Colour some flower paste golden yellow, roll into a ball then into a long thin cone. Stick your dowel into the thicker end of the cone. Cut six petals and remove from dowel. Squash, pinch and pull each petal. Take a piece of 30-gauge covered dark green wire, make a hook and slide down the throat. Place a single white stamen into the throat (refer to picture below for positioning). To make the buds, roll a thin cone, stick the hooked wire into the thin end, cut approximately one-third of the way down with scissors and then twist the two pieces together like a spiral.

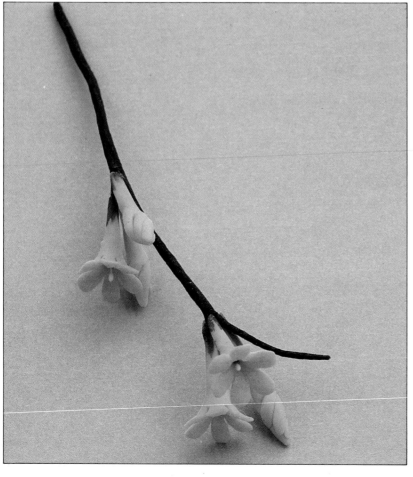

### Finishing

Dilute some dark green, paste food colouring with clear spirit and paint calyxes on each of the flowers and buds using a small, fine paintbrush and leave to dry. Tape the flowers and buds in clumps on to a piece of 26-gauge wire which then acts as the main stem.

Winter jasmine is a most attractive flower to use in winter sprays and contrasts with the usual red and green Christmas cake spray.

# Daisy

Take a small ball of white paste, mould into a cone, press a dowel into the thicker end. Cut eight petals, and open up the flower. Squash, pinch and pull each petal then pinch each one in to a slight point. Make a hook on a piece of 28-gauge dark green wire, dip in egg white and thread down the throat of the flower. Take a piece of dark yellow paste, roll into a tiny ball and holding it on your first finger, press some tulle over the top, to flatten and mark it. Remove the tulle and insert into the centre of the daisy with the patterned edge uppermost. Using a small calyx cutter, cut out some thin green paste. Thread up the wire and stick this onto the flower.

### Finishing

Dust a little green petal dust into the centre of the daisy. Daisies are an attractive flower to use on many types of cake and are particularly suitable for spring or summer weddings.

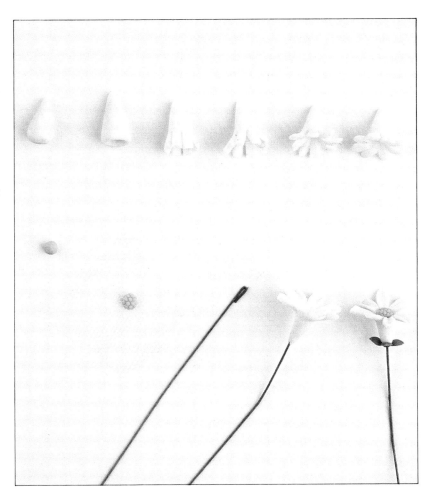

# Primrose

Colour some paste to a creamy lemon-colour, roll into a ball then into a long cone with a slightly bulbous end. Stick a dowel into the bulbous end, cut five petals then make a further five cuts in the centre of each petal but half the length of the first cuts. Open up and you will have five heart-shaped petals. Run a cocktail stick over the surface of each petal. Make a hook on a piece of 26-gauge mid-green wire and thread through the throat of the flower. Place a small ball of green paste into the centre of the flower and using a cocktail stick, make a small hole in the centre of the green piece and use to position a white stamen. Roll out some green paste and cut a calyx using a mini 8-petal daisy, cup on a piece of sponge and thread up the wire. Stick around the base of the flower squashing around the base.

### Finishing

Dust a little green into the centre of the flowers. To make a stem more in scale with the flower, two additional wires are taped to the original one. Primroses are ideal for spring cakes, particularly Easter cakes or country-style weddings.

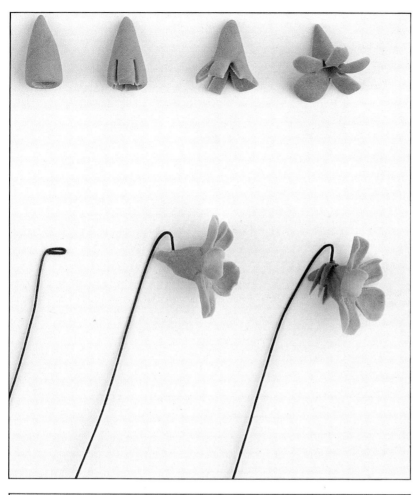

# Violet

Colour some paste violet and roll into a ball. Mould into a cone and stick a dowel into the thicker end of the cone. Cut one petal to a quarter of the total circumference of the paste and four petals from the remaining three-quarters. Open up the flower and run a cocktail stick over each petal in turn. Make a hook in a piece of 28-gauge green wire then bend a hook at right angles, as shown and dip the hook in egg white. Thread the wire through the throat and push so that the wire pierces the top of the back of the cone behind the top two petals, making sure that the larger single petal is at the bottom. Cut off any excess paste and then bend back the wire. Roll out some green paste, cut a diamond shape and then cut each side almost in half to make the calyx. Place over the violet as shown. Make an orange stamen and insert into the centre of the violet. Mark a vein down the centre of the large petal.

**Finishing**

Dust with dark violet petal dust. Mix a little white petal dust with some clear spirit and paint a few lines into the centre of the violet.

Violets are a common flower connected with springtime and Easter. They look attractive on Easter cakes, eggs and birthday cakes.

# Heartsease

Colour some paste to a pale ivory-colour and roll into a ball. Form into a cone shape and stick a dowel into the thicker end of the cone. Cut one petal from a quarter of the cone and four equal petals out of the remaining three-quarters. Squash and pinch but do not pull each petal, then roll a cocktail stick quite firmly over the surface to thin out rather than to frill the petals. Place on the wire in the same way as for the violet. Squash to elongate the petals and to push up the top layer. Once on the wire insert a small ball of paste into the centre and make a cavity in it using a small ball tool or the end of a glass-headed pin. Tuck the bottom of the large petal under to make it into a heart shape. The calyx is the same as for the violet.

**Finishing**

Dust the top two petals mauve or violet and the other three yellow, the backs should be dusted in the same colours. Put a touch of mauve and violet on the bottom petal for detail. Mix some black paste colouring with some clear spirit and paint the central lines using a very fine brush. To finish, dust a little green into the centre of the flower.

Heartsease is a wild pansy and comes in a range of colours. They are dainty colourful flowers making them suitable for many types of cakes and sprays.

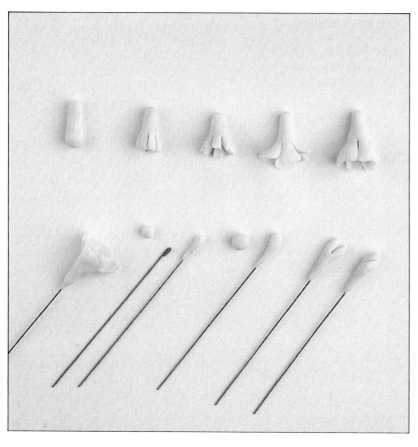

# Freesia

Make a dumbell shape in ivory paste and stick a dowel into one end. Cut into six equal petals; squash, pinch and pull and roll a cocktail stick over each petal. Place onto a piece of sponge and cup each one stroking the ball tool from the outside to the inside of the flower. Push your ball or dog bone tool down the centre of the throat to stretch it slightly. Take a piece of 26-gauge mid-green wire, hook and dip in egg white and thread through the throat. Take a small ball of paste and place inside the flower to act like a plug to stop it from sliding down the wire. Using a cocktail stick make a small hole in the plug and fold together three 2.5cm (1in) pieces of cotton or stamen cotton and push the folded ends into the hole using the thumb and first fingers of both hands squash slightly. Move three alternate petals inwards and others outwards, squash just below the petals. To make sure the centre three stay in position, the outer three are then gently eased up to sit as a second row on top of the first three petals.

The buds are made in various sizes, the smallest are just tiny cones placed on wire and rolled down between the fingers to form a long, elegant bud. The twisted buds are made in the same way as the winter jasmine buds.

### Finishing

Once dry, dust with pink or any other appropriate petal dust, as freesias come in a wide range of colours. A little green petal dust is brushed into the centre and around the base of the flower. The buds are lightly dusted all over with green while the twisted buds are half green and half pink. You will need graduated flowers as well as buds to make a spray.

Mix a little green food colouring with some clear spirit and paint a calyx on each bud and flower. Paint a small single leaf shape on either side using a fine paintbrush and allow to dry. Assemble starting with the smallest bud and placing the others to the right then to the left all the way down.

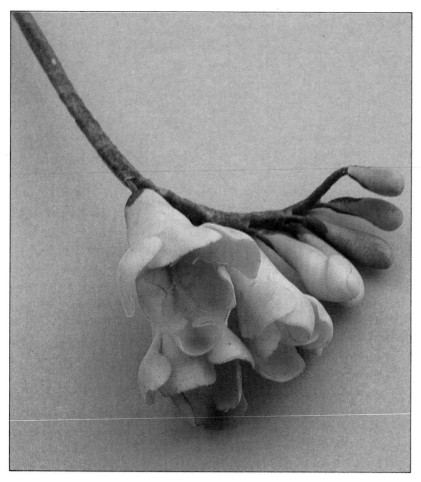

# Snowdrop

Roll a small ball of white paste and make into a cone, then stick a dowel into the thicker end and cut six petals. While still on the stick, make a smaller cut in the centre of three alternate petals as for the primrose. The three smaller petals are a smaller version of the primrose. Squash, pinch and pull all of the petals, roll a cocktail stick over each of them. Cup both sets of petals on a foam base. Stick a ball tool into the centre and roll the flower about to make a bulbous cavity above the petals. Make a hook on a piece of 30-gauge dark green wire and thread through the flower; bend over so the snowdrop hangs like a bell. Slide a small ball of paste along the wire for the calyx, sticking in position with egg white. The three heart-shaped petals sit in the centre, with the three large plain ones on top similar to the petal formation of the freesia. Roll out some green paste and cut a thin pointed strip, stick the square end on to the wire and mould around the base of the flowers.

**Finishing**
Mix some green colouring with clear spirit and paint some very fine feathery lines on to the three heart-shaped petals. The snowdrop being so very small is the most fiddly flower to make and only practice will enable you to manipulate tiny petals.

Snowdrops have a limited use, but look very attractive on a winter or early spring wedding cake, especially if the wedding is in a white and green colour scheme.

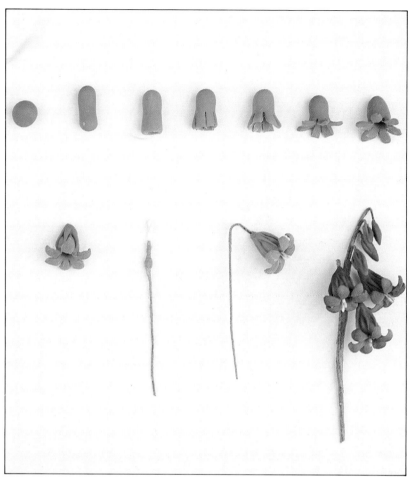

# Bluebell

Colour some paste bluish-mauve and roll into a ball. Mould into a dumbell shape, stick a dowel into one end and cut six petals. Place each petal onto a piece of sponge and cup using a ball tool stick, then insert a ball tool up into the centre of the flower to make a bulbous cavity. Using tweezers, pinch the flower as shown to produce a ribbed effect on the side. Tape two white stamen ends onto a piece of wire, and wrap round extra tape to stop the wire coming back through the flower. Thread the wire and stamens through the flower. The buds are made by making a small cone, pinched with tweezers.

**Finishing**
Brush with a mixture of blue and violet dusting powder. Tape the buds and flowers onto a main stem as shown starting with a bud in the centre then setting another to the left then the next to the right and so on. You can make a long spray by using five to seven buds and five to seven flowers. Bluebells look attractive bunched together with other spring flowers.

Many dozens of flowers can be made using the techniques shown and once the technique is mastered you should be able to look at almost any flower and be able to make it by deciding which of the skills will be necessary to use. The flowers covered in this chapter may be used in a wide variety of sprays and floral arrangements. The following provide just a few ideas to get you started.

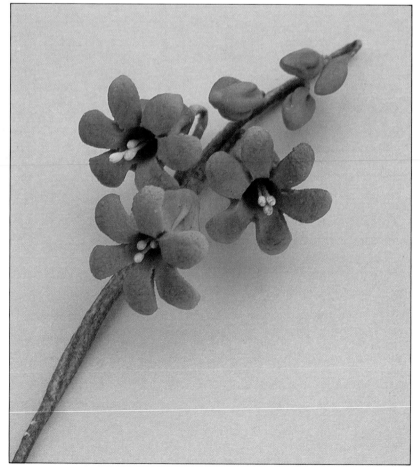

## Baby's Booties

A pair of small china baby's booties filled with pastel-tipped petal blossom would be a suitable gift for a new arrival or for a christening cake. Fill the booties with white sugarpaste; make some figure-of-eight double loops in lemon and white. Place the ribbons in position then arrange an assortment of sizes of basic five petal blossom and buds in the booties using a pair of tweezers. Tie two lemon bows and stick these on to the front of the booties with royal icing or a rubber based glue.

## Posy of Pulled Blossoms

A posy of pulled flowers would make a delightful decoration on any cake and could be made in a variety of colour combinations. For this posy you will need fifteen to twenty five-petal blossoms and about eight buds and frilled blossoms. When dry, these have been dusted with blue and peach petal dust and arranged with blue and peach 6mm (¼in) figure-of-eight double ribbon loops and placed into a small, white post holder. For instructions on wiring flowers into a spray refer to page 236 which covers the posy wiring technique step-by-step.

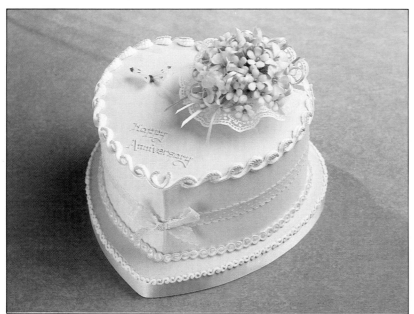

## Peach and Blue Anniversary Cake

The same peach and blue posy on an Anniversary Cake. The cake is a 20cm (8in) heart-shaped and royal-iced in peach with shells and running S scrolls piped with a No42 tube then with a No2 and overpiped in blue using a No1 tube. A blue polka dot ribbon has been attached around the side with a bow on the front. An inscription, a small feather butterfly and the posy finish the top decoration.

## Silver Vase

This flowing vase is filled with dozens of pulled blossoms and buds. Make five identical legs and wire into a posy with double figure-of-eight loops and stick into a silver vase. This would be an ideal top decoration for a three tier wedding cake. (refer to Lesson 19 for information on wiring flowers into posies. The principle is like the reverse S or crescent spray).

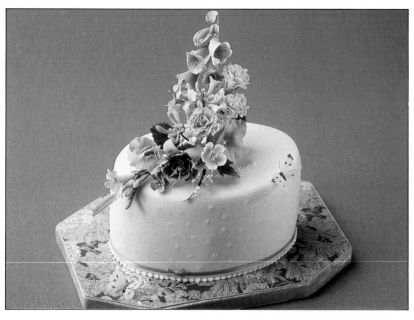

## Garden and Wayside Cake

Cover a long octagonal board with wild silk or an alternative fabric. The edge has been finished with a velvet ribbon around it. Cover a small oval cake in pink sugarpaste. Transfer on to the board with an oval piece of waxed paper between the cake and board so as not to strain the fabric, making it possible to reuse the board. Pipe a small shell around the base. A 3mm (1/8in) ribbon is placed above the shell and then forget-me-nots are piped freehand over the sides of the cake. A spray of flowers is placed into posy pick with a butterfly and inscription to finish off this unusual floral cake.

# Cutter Flowers

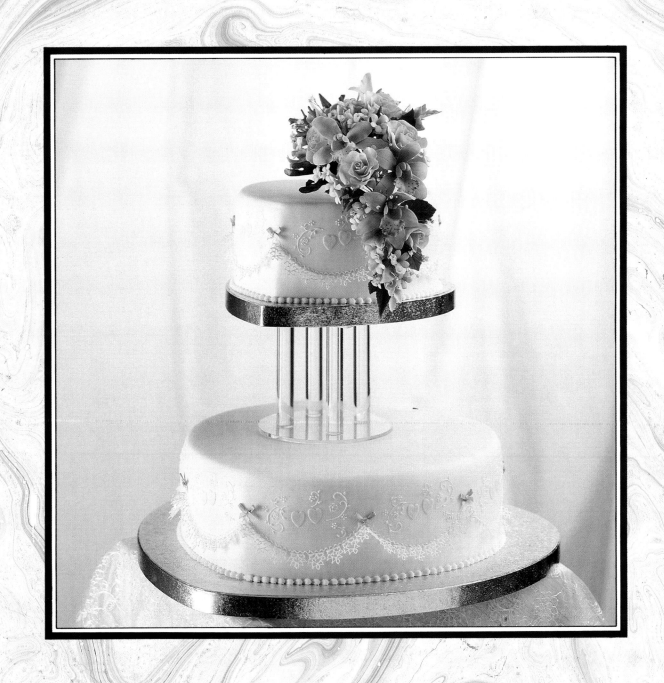

# Flowers Made Using Cutters

Numerous varieties of flowers may be made from the many cutters now on the market. Cutters for flowers and foliage come in lots of sizes and makes, some metal and some plastic. Every manufacturer produces a slightly different shaped cutter for the same flower and they all make slightly different looking flowers. For some of the flowers shown, you will have to modify the shape of a cutter.

## The Rose

The rose, symbol of eternal love, peace and serenity, is the most popular cutter flower. The one shown here works equally well as a three, four or five level petal formation.

**Method**
Colour some flower paste to the required colour, here peach has been used. For the best results prepare graduated shades of the colour, use the darkest shade at the centre and lighter shades for the outer petals. If matching pastes to bridal fabrics, match your darkest shade paste to the fabric.

Roll the paste into a ball, then into a cone. Make a hook on a piece of 26-gauge mid-green wire, dip into egg white and stick into the thick end of the cone. Mould around the base to cover up the hole. Leave to dry for a day.

Roll out some paste until it is translucent, cut six petals. The cutters shown come in a set of five, the middle three cutters of the set have been used to make the rose shown, the first six petals have been cut with the second smallest cutter. Brush some egg white on the top of the cone, place the first petal like a peep bonnet on to the cone, tuck the left-hand side in and wrap the right-hand side on top of this.

Continue the second row by placing another petal on the join of the first petal, stick with a little egg white, leaving the right-hand side of the petal open. The next petal sits inside the last and overlaps on top of the neighbouring petal, so now there is one petal in the centre and two petals on the next row. Continue on to the next row, this time

adding three petals. Place in an overlap formation creating a spiral appearance. The first six petals are now in position, no frilling or softening of petals is needed for the first six petals. Do not try to cover the cone, if you look at the picture the petals only come about two thirds of the way down the cone.

Lighten the paste by adding white paste to a ratio of two parts coloured paste to one part white. Remember if you are making more than one rose, place the first six petals on all your roses before adding white to the paste. Roll out some of the lighter paste, cut four petals using a slightly larger cutter, soften these four slightly using a cocktail stick, position these petals using an overlap, spiral formation.

Add further white paste to the peach for the final row. Roll out the paste, cut five petals with the next cutter up in size, frill with a cocktail stick and attach. Usually you will have to do this with the rose hanging upside-down so the petals do not flop back.

Take a piece of green paste, make

into a cone with a flattened bottom and place a piece of flattened white paste beneath this, as shown.
Roll out using a paintbrush as a mini rolling-pin and cut out using a calyx cutter. Cut feathers on the legs, as shown, turn over and, using a large ball tool, make a cavity for the rose to sit in. Slide up the wire, sticking with egg white and mould into the rose.

To make the leaves, squash a piece of green paste and roll out retaining a thicker area. Cut out with the thickest area at the base of the leaf. Hold firmly between your thumb and first finger and insert a piece of hooked wire. Press into a veiner; roll a cocktail stick along the edge and clearly mark the central vein. Support in a natural position until completely dry.

Dust with a mixture of brown and yellow petal dust. When dry, dust the rose with a peach and pink mixture when dry to lift it slightly. The rose and leaves are then wired together to form a spray.

Roll out some paste but do not roll it until it is translucent as you would for the rose, as for double frilling it should be a fraction thicker. Cut out the carnation shape using the carnation cutter.

Using a sharp modelling knife, cut on the indentation and two or three times on the curve of each scallop. To frill the petal, take a cocktail stick and working with a firm rolling movement, start frilling the paste keeping it moving all the time so that it does not stick to the work surface. Continue until frilled all the way around. Turn over onto a piece of thin foam, brush egg white all over the surface up to the frilling.

Thread the wire through the centre, fold in half, remove from sponge, brush egg white over the centre third of one side and bring the left-hand side third over; repeat on the other side by turning it over and bring from the side to the centre so it is an S shape if looked at from above. Squash firmly onto the wire.

Continue by rolling, cutting and frilling two further petals. These are turned over, brushed with egg white and slid onto the wire. Hang upside-down supporting between your two thumbs and first fingers. Squash all around to get an even finish.

Make a small cone, known as a Mexican hat, rolling from the inside to the outside using a paintbrush. Cut out a calyx and then, as for pulled flowers, stick a wooden dowel down the centre to open it up. Slide this up the wire and attach to the carnation with egg white.

To make the bud, surround a yellow cone with a piece of green paste and cut through the green using a modelling knife to reveal the yellow underneath. Place onto a piece of wire. Dust the petals with a flat brush using a contrasting colour and wire with the bud into a spray.

## Spray Carnation

Spray carnations are a very lovely, delicate flower to use on any celebration or wedding cake and can be finished in some interesting colour combinations.

### Method
Take a piece of 26-gauge mid-green wire, put a hook on one end and hook a piece of cotton or thread on to this, squash with pliers and wrap a piece of fine rose wire around the top piece. Using a thin piece of floristry tape, wrap around the top and tape down to the base of the wire.

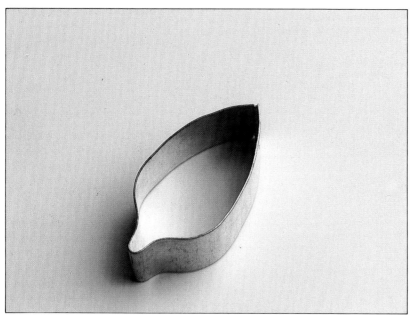

# Clematis

The clematis is an attractive climber. The one illustrated is Montana, a small four petalled variety that flowers in abundance. There are many books on clematis or look in a seed catalogue as these usually include full colour pictures of clematis and other flowers. Clematis would be very dramatic on a wedding cake and, as many men grow them, could be used on a man's cake along with the foliage.

*The cutter for Clematis Montana is made by squashing a Christmas Rose cutter. Only bend cutters if you plan to do the flowers on a regular basis, if not use a cardboard or petal template, (see page 227).*

**Method**

Roll out some pink paste and cut four petals. Place on a veiner like a violet leaf, hibiscus, or any with fan-shape veining. Turn over and using a veining tool or cocktail stick, mark two curved lines then turn over so the lines are underneath and inverted on the top.

Take a small, circular piece of paste and make a hole in it. With the end of a paintbrush, squash slightly and sit inside a wooden curtain ring. Assemble the four petals onto the tiny centre ring sticking with egg white and using the curtain ring as a support. Stick some white stamen cotton pieces around the centre. These have been dusted a mauve colour in places to produce a striped effect.

Take some yellow cotton, wrap round the tweezer ends that should be about 12mm (½in) apart, wind around 13 times and then twist some wire around the centre to form a figure-of-eight with the wire in the centre. Cut the two loops and trim off the excess wire and stick into the centre of the clematis to make the mass of yellow in the centre. Allow to dry before finishing. Dust with a stripe of darker pink down the centre of each petal and dust a little green around the base of the petals.

# Petunia

Petunias with their floppy flowers come in many colours, including pink, mauve, lilac, red and striped effect ones. They would be nice on a summer birthday or get well cake because they are a cheery flower.

**Method**
Make a cone and place flat end on to work surface; roll using a paintbrush until you have a central node and a refined outer area. Cut out using a petunia cutter. Place a wooden dowel into the centre of the flower and rotate it to stretch the throat open. Holding the back of the flower, place each petal down on to a leaf veiner to vein the petals, then holding on the edge of your work surface, frill the petal edges with a cocktail stick. Tape five white stamens together with floristry tape; make a hole at the base of the flower and stick the stamen piece into the throat threading through the back. If making an unwired petunia, trim off the excess stamen ends once the flower is dry. If wiring the petunia, slide a small hollowed cone of green on to the back and tape the stamens to a piece of wire with mid-green floristry tape. Dust with two shades of pink to get a striped effect with a little green in the centre.

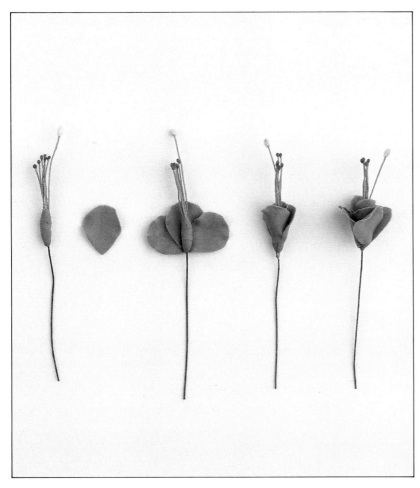

# Fuchsia

Fuchsia are a dramatic summer garden flower hanging in clumps like ballerinas in the sunshine. They come in hundreds of colours. It is best to pick some real fuchsias to achieve naturalistic colouring, or have a book with colour photographs at hand. For the best effects, show them hanging out of a vase as they do naturally.

**Method**

Take six stamens in dark pink with one longer than the other five. Wrap a piece of 28-gauge green wire around them. Squash a piece of paste around the wire and a piece of paste on the longer stamen. Roll out some paste and cut six petals using a rose petal cutter. Lay three in a fan, sticking with egg white. There are ten wrapped around the small cone of paste. Stick the further three petals, after frilling them slightly, overlapping the joins in the first row of petals. Roll out some more paste and, using a pansy sepal cutter, cut out four petals. Put on to a veiner to give some detail to the petals. Roll a cocktail stick over the edge to frill them. Place the four on as shown. Make a Mexican hat shape in a second colour, rolling with a paintbrush, and cut out the back piece of the flower using a fuchsia sepal cutter. Vein each petal and cup upwards on a piece of foam. Make a cavity in the centre for the first stage to sit into; slide the prepared centre up through the back piece sticking with egg white. Stick a calyx on to the back, and dust according to colour scheme and also dust the long stigma green. Tape on to a piece of 26-gauge wire for support if wiring several into a spray.

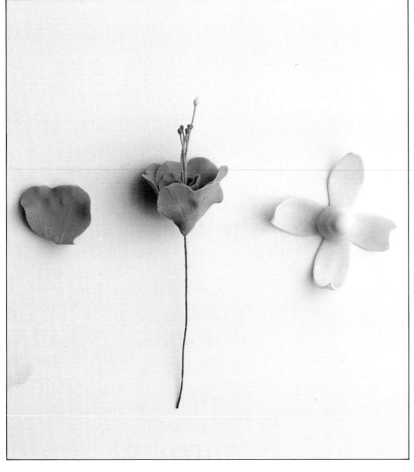

# Sweet Pea

Sweet peas are a very popular garden summer flower. They come in a lovely assortment of pastel shades as well as dark velvety colours. They can be made in a white or pale cream and dusted or painted in a colour.

## Method

Take a small pea of paste. Hook a piece of 26-gauge mid-green wire and stick the pea of paste on to the hook that has been dipped in egg white. Flatten the pea of paste slightly. Roll out some paste and cut out a rose petal using the second smallest petal in the rose set. Place on to a piece of sponge, brush a little egg white down the centre and down one side of the petal. Then with the point of the petal towards you, take the flattened piece of paste on the wire and place the thin edge into the centre of the petal; fold both sides over and squash together. Pull the top piece back at a slight right angle.

Roll out some more paste and cut out the first main petal. Roll a cocktail stick around the petal to frill, place on a piece of sponge and vein the centre. Place the prepared wired inner petal into the centre of the main petal with the tiny right angled piece hooked over the top gap in the petal. Squash at the back as shown. Roll out a little more paste, cut out the second main petal and shape. Frill this slightly, put on a piece of foam, vein the centre then turn over so the veining is inverted. Stick the prepared piece to this new petal using egg white. As the sepals start to set you can move them about. Roll out some green paste, cut out a calyx. Place on a piece of sponge, cup and slide up the wire, sticking with egg white. The tendrils are made by wrapping pieces of wire around the handle of a paintbrush. Dust when dry and assemble into a spray.

Sweet peas tend to look best on their own because they are flat flowers. They do not mix well. A natural type of bunch arrangement suits them best.

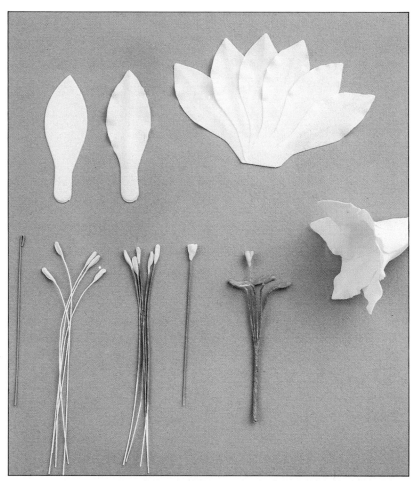

# Longiflorum Lily

These elegant trumpet-shaped lilies look very attractive on a large wedding cake.

**Method**
Roll out some white paste and cut six petals using a lily cutter. Soften each petal slightly using a cocktail stick; vein on the reverse side of the petal. Stick with a little egg white into a fan shape. Roll into a hollow cake pillar to dry. This is ideal to support the shape of the lily. For the stamens and stigma make a hook in a piece of 26-gauge Nile green wire; take five lily stamens and use fine pieces of floristry tape to cover the white cotton underneath but leave the lemon top exposed. The stigma has a small cone attached to the top and is divided into thirds. Brush the lemon lily stamens with egg white and dip in dark yellow or gold petal dust; leave to dry. Bend the stamens with tweezers and tape all five in a ring to the longer stigma. Once the lily is dry, slot through the lily base – if wiring, tape the end of stamen arrangement to a 24-gauge wire and slide a small ball of green paste up the wire to fill in the end of the lily. Dust with green in the form of lines down the centre of each petal.

# Cymbidium Orchid

Cymbidiums come in hundreds of colours and various shapes. A medium sized cutter was used to make an orchid suitable for use in a corsage or in a large spray. The step-by-step assembly of the Cymbidium orchid is covered on page 242. Cymbidiums are popular in autumn wedding bouquets

## Method

Roll out some paste retaining a thicker part as for leaves. Cut out a petal and insert a hooked piece of 30-gauge wire, vein on a sweetcorn leaf or other suitable veiner. Three large and two Cymbidium. One large sepal is set against a piece of dowel or tube, the other four sepals, two large, two smaller, are all laid over the curved surface. Leave to dry. To make the throat, hook a piece of 26-gauge wire and place a medium cone with a bulbous end on the wire. Roll out two small wing shapes using a paintbrush handle. Make a small cut with scissors underneath each wing and vein both sides along the length of the column. Bend over, make a small cavity and place a tiny, yellow ball split in half in position sticking with egg white. Roll out some green paste, cut out the throat petal, then cut two small pieces out with a modelling knife as shown. Frill the scalloped end of the petal only, then cup the two side sections of the petal on a piece of foam. Vein the centre using a veining tool. Brush a little egg white at the base of the petal and place the column in position. Wrap the sides of the petal over to meet, then stick the throat petal about one third of the way up the column. Place a small piece of foam rubber into the throat to stop it collapsing while drying, (this has been removed from the photograph to show the detail).

Place on an orchid former, or support on a piece of foam rubber allowing the orchid to hang over the edge. Leave all parts to dry. The assemble and finishing is covered in depth on page 242.

# Cattleya Orchid

The Cattleya orchid, known as the bridal orchid in America, comes in shades of cream, pink, mauve, lemon and white highlighted with various pastel colours; it is a very feminine orchid with its frilly petals and is always a popular choice. The assembly of the Cattleya is identical to that of the Cymbidium.

### Method

Roll out some white paste using a paintbrush, retaining a thicker part at one end. Cut three long, thin petals and two that are slightly shorter and wider. The thin ones have a deep, wide veining on the backs of the petals; one is set-off against the tubing and the two wider petals are both frilled and veined and set-off over a curve. All of these petals go on 30-gauge green wire.

Begin the throat by making a column, which is shorter than that for the Cymbidium. Vein down both sides. Make a small yellow ball and cut in half, this is then placed into a small cavity. The throat petal is cut out and veined on any fan formation leaf veiner, alternatively you can buy orchid throat veiners. Frill all the way around. Place the throat petal on a piece of sponge rubber and position the column at the base of the petal, yellow ball side downwards; bring both sides up to meet at the top sticking with egg white. Support in an orchid throat former or over the edge of some thick foam. Dust with a pale pink and lemon petal dust.

*Cutters for the Cattleya orchid.*

# Miniature Cymbidium

Miniature Cymbidiums look very delicate on a tiny birthday cake or in a spray as a filler in conjunction with larger orchids. They are quite fiddly and quite time consuming to make.

**Method**

Make a tiny hook on a piece of 28-gauge wire. Place a small cone on one end, graduate its shape to form a bulbous tip. Vein on both sides, then bend the top over slightly. Roll out some pink paste and cut the throat petal. Frill the bottom edge and cup the two sides, then attach to the prepared column with egg white as shown. The sepals on this type of cutter are all in one; roll out some pink paste and cut out the petals. Vein each one down the centre. Cup one petal, then turn over and cup the other four, when you turn the petal over again they will curve backwards. Slide the throat into the centre of the petal sticking with a little egg white; leave until dry. Dust with a darker pink and paint a few delicate spots using petal dust mixed with clear spirit.

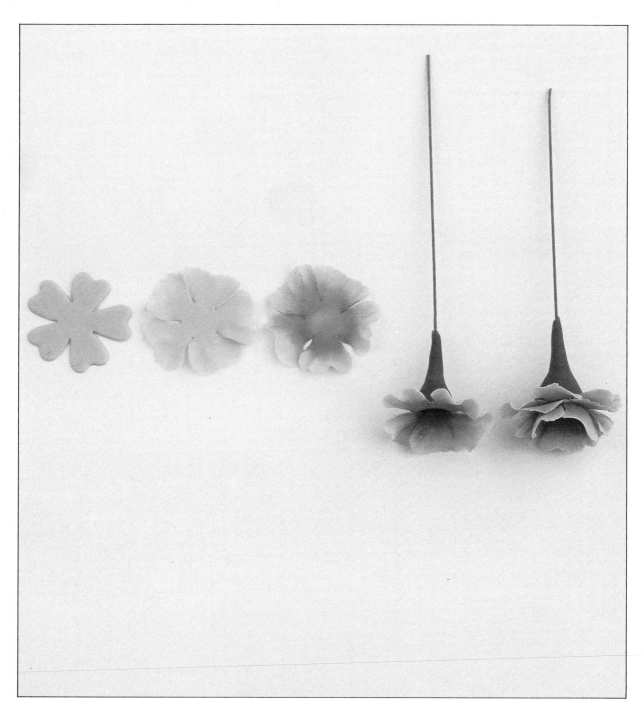

## Doris Pink

Doris pinks are a popular flower especially with the older generation. They are a mid-summer flower and part of the Dianthus family. Pinks can be used like carnations in sprays or used in a natural bunch on a cake tied in a bow with a piece of ribbon. Using the smaller cutter you can make French marigolds using the same method.

**Method**

Hook a piece of 25-gauge Nile green wire; make a medium-sized cone of green paste. Dip in egg white and insert the wire into the finer end of the cone. Make a cavity in the top of the cone for

the petals. Roll out some pink paste and using a medium primrose cutter, cut out the petal, make a few tiny cuts around

each petal and frill with a cocktail stick. Dust with dark pink powder straight away. Brush a little egg white into the cavity of the calyx, place the first petal in position and repeat with a further three or four petals until the flower is finished. The centre petal should be squashed up to fill the centre cavity.

## Marigold

Use the cutter which is the next size down to the Doris pink and use dark, yellow paste with orange dust. The calyx has tweezer pinches down it and has a touch of burgundy petal dust put on when dry.

# Gypsophila

Gypsophila is a dainty flower favoured by many brides for their bouquets. Making these tiny flowers in flower paste is very time consuming, but worth the trouble, it softens harsh flowers and fills in sprays beautifully.

As it is almost impossible to tape wires successfully to such a dainty skeleton of branches, it is better to place the sugar buds and blossoms onto real gypsophila stems.

## Method

Buy a piece of gypsophila and dry by hanging in a dry place for 3-4 days. Alternatively, place sprigs in the microwave on defrost setting for about 3-4 minutes. This draws the moisture out, it then only needs a day of hanging. When dry, the flowers will be

crispy to the touch. Cut these all off so you are left with just the stems. Roll tiny balls of white paste and stick on to some of the branches. Most of the

branches are in threes so you can use either two buds and one flower or two flowers and one bud on each. Roll out some white paste, cut out two flowers at a time using a small blossom ejector cutter; cut each scallop of the petal in half and frill the whole blossom like a miniature carnation.

Take two cut, frilled blossoms, stick together with egg white and make a tiny hole in the centre. Using a cocktail stick, thread on to the end of a stem, as with the spray carnation, fold in half like a fan, then into an S shape. Squash with tweezers. Continue all over the sprig of stems covering with flowers. This size spray would take about 30 minutes to complete. When finished, dry for a while then mix some green paste colouring with some clear spirit and paint the calyxes on each bud and flower with a fine paintbrush.

# Ivy Leaf

Ivy leaves are a useful foliage suitable for year round use. They are, however, particularly useful for Christmas cakes. The ones shown are variegated ivy but the principle is the same for all foliage.

**Method**

Take a piece of pale ivory–coloured paste and roll into a ball. Squash, and roll with a paintbrush, retaining a thicker part at one end for the wire. Cut out the ivy leaf positioning the base at thicker part as shown; hold firmly between your thumb and first finger

and insert a 28-gauge green wire that has first been hooked and dipped in egg white. Place on an ivy leaf or violet leaf veiner or use a real ivy leaf. Vein on both sides. Run a cocktail stick over the edge to soften slightly. Place on a sponge and vein the centre of the leaf using a veining tool or cocktail stick. Pinch the bottom slightly and leave to dry. When dry, dust the back green, then work the variegation by using two shades of green. Brush the lighter shade on first using a flat paintbrush and brushing from the centre to the outside of the leaf, then using a darker shade, dust on top of the lighter colour, again working from the centre outwards.

## Periwinkle

The periwinkle has been made in the same way as the variegated ivy using the same cutter as clematis, but the green has been painted on by mixing green colouring with spirit. Start off with a very pale green for the background, slowly build up the colour with two stronger shades. Dry before using.

## Foliage

Here several varieties of foliage have been made in the same way as the ivy. They have been coloured in various shades of green either by dusting, painting or varnishing to show the different effects.

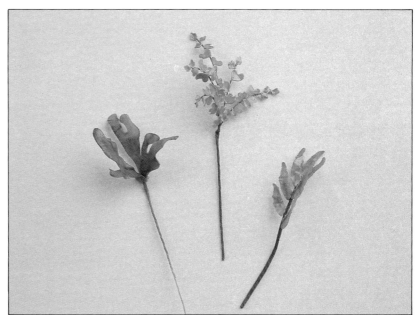

## Ferns

This picture shows sword and maidenhair fern. Make a wire skeleton and cut out the leaf shapes, stick on with softened flower paste which acts like strong glue. Dust or paint green.

# Heart-shaped Wedding Cake

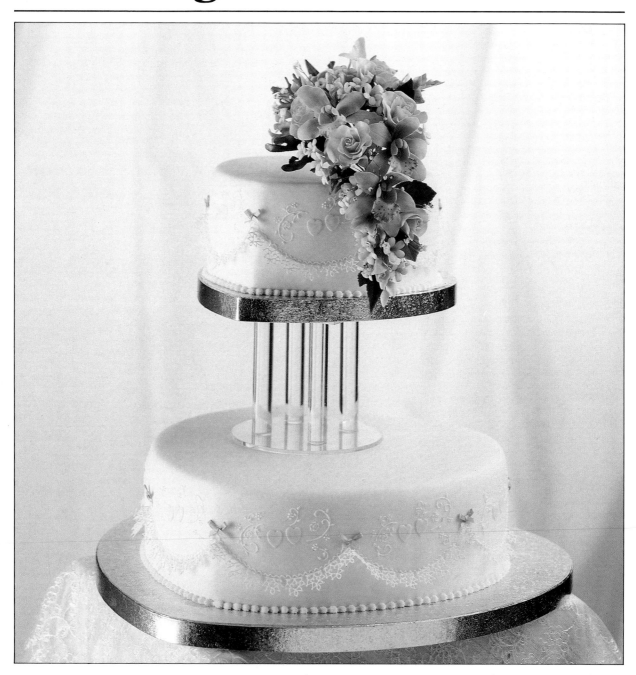

This elegant cake with its spray of roses and Cymbidium orchids is shown step by step on page 245.

**Instructions**

Marzipan and cover a 25 and 15cm (10 and 6in) heart cake. Place on boards and leave for a few days. During this time the flowers can be made and assembled and the lace pieces piped. Make a paper pattern for the side by measuring from the front point to the back. Fold the strip in four and draw an equal scallop in each division, scribe onto both sides of the cake to end up with eight scallops in total. The embroidery may be worked free-hand but the shaping could be included in the original pattern and scribed on at the same time as the scallops. Stick the tiny cutout hearts onto the cake using a little egg white. Pipe a shell around the base with a No42 tube then pipe a scalloped line along the scribed line and attach the lace, place the miniature bows above the points. Using a posy pick stick, make a hole into the top tier and place the spray into position, (page 247). This cake has a perspex cake divider instead of traditional pillars.

# Wild Flowers

# Wild Flowers

**M**aking wild flowers allows all your creative instincts to come into play. There are very few cutters available, so it is a matter of experimenting with the different principles you have learnt to create the flowers of your choice.

Use the flowers in this lesson as guidelines to get you started. However, if you are starting from scratch you will find it essential to have either a real flower model to hand, or detailed photographs or illustrations of the anatomy of the flower in question. When looking at the flower you wish to model, try to imagine other flowers that are similarly constructed and if these are covered in this book, then you will know which method to follow.

Honeysuckle is made using the finger flower method. As this is quite an advanced flower, you have to work quickly to complete before the long sepal dries. First attempts may be disappointing because the petal starts to dry before all stages are finished, but with practice you will become quicker.

## Honeysuckle

Wild honeysuckle in soft tones of cream, yellow and pale orange grows freely in the hedgerows in the summer months. It can be used in amongst other flowers or on its own. For a dramatic effect use a spray of three or four pieces of honeysuckle trailing over the edge of the cake.

**1.** Using ivory flower paste start off with the sprocks in the centre. Take three pieces of 30-gauge green wire, put hooks on both ends of two pieces and just on one end of the third. Dip the hooks in egg white then place a tiny cone of paste on each. Use the end of a paintbrush, as shown, to make a cavity in the thicker end of each cone to expose the tip of the wire.

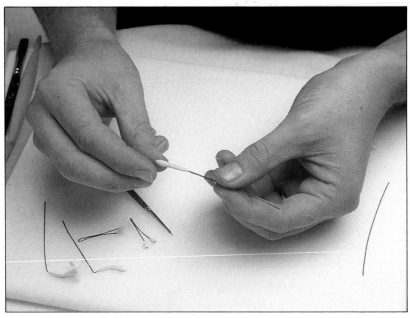

**2.** To make the buds, make hooks on five to seven pieces of 30-gauge wire. Roll a ball of paste into a long thin cone and then stick onto the first hook, roll between your two first fingers to get a long elegant bud bringing the top to a slight point.

212

**3.** Taking the bud in between your thumb and first finger, curve both the bud and wire gently. Take a pair of tweezers, bend at the neck as shown. You will need to repeat steps 2 to 3 with the remaining buds, but graduate the size of the buds to finish with three or four different sizes.

**4.** Take a piece of paste and roll into a long thin cone. Using a satay stick, insert this into the thicker end, as for pulled and finger flowers, and rotate the stick so it moves freely.

**5.** Cut a thin strip to form a petal by cutting two straight lines near each other then make a slight angled cut either side of this as shown. The remaining piece is cut into four. This is clearer in picture 7.

**6.** Open up the flower by bending each petal backwards. Roll a cocktail stick on each of the four top petals to frill them slightly.

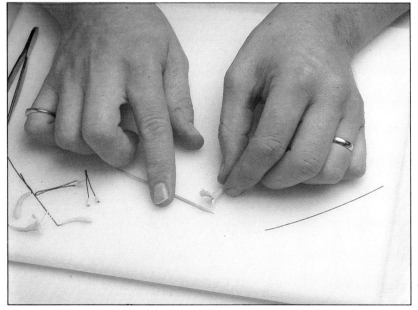

**7.** Roll the single petal to approximately twice its original length using a cocktail stick, be very gentle as too much pressure will cause the petal to break.

**8.** Curl petal under using a ball tool. Make a hook on a piece of 30-gauge wire and thread down through throat of the flower.

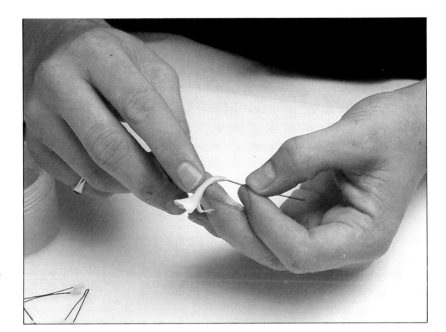

**9.** Roll between your fingers to make a long tubular back; lay over a wooden dowel with the single long petal downwards, and push on top with your finger curving the flower and wire at the same time.

**10.** Take three double fine white stamens, fold two in half and one irregularly to end up with five the same length and one longer one. Run a pair of scissors along the cotton to curl them slightly, then insert into the centre of the flower with tweezers. If you do not have fine stamens, use button-thread instead.

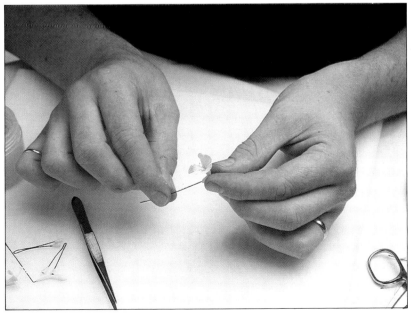

**11.** Squash the centre to make sure the stamens are secure. To make a spray, you will need three to five flowers.

To make a spray, you will need three to five flowers.

## Finishing

Dust with a soft, round brush and a mixture of orange and yellow petal dust to produce the soft apricot tones. Dust the longest stamen, the centre of the flower, and base of the flower soft green. The buds are dusted green at the base and yellow at the top. The sprocks are dusted green. Tape the two folded sprocks into the single one then, working in a clockwise movement, gradually increase the size of the buds as you progress. Finish off by placing the flower in position as shown.

# Foxgloves

These tall flowers with their hanging heads are an excellent way to give height to a spray. They are made without cutters so it will take a little practise to produce a consistent shape, however, the sizes need to be graduated to be most effective.

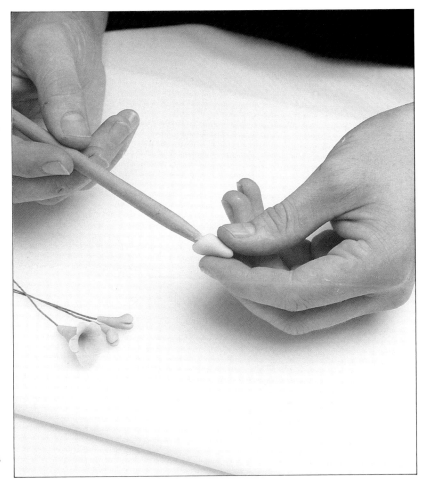

**1.** Mould a piece of creamy pink paste into a cone with a sloped side, insert a wooden dowel into the end and rotate so that the stick moves freely.

**2.** Cut one petal from one-quarter of the circumference and the remaining three-quarters into four equal petals, just like the heartsease; squash, pinch and pull each petal.

**3.** Roll a cocktail stick along each petal to thin rather than to frill.

**4.** Stick a ball tool into the throat of the flower to open it up slightly.

**5.** Using a dog bone tool on sponge, stretch the throat of the foxglove so it cups slightly.

**6.** Make a hook on a piece of wire and taking a piece of floristry tape wrap over the hook and tape down the wire.

**7.** Thread down through the flower, the thicker end piece stops the wire coming right through the foxglove flower.

**8.** To finish the foxglove, dust with pink dusting powder. A white petal dust is dusted on the inside of the flower. Mix some burgundy petal dust with some clear spirit and paint the spots on the throat.

# Blackberries

Blackberries are a very attractive late summer or autumn fruit wired in a spray, as shown. They look most appealing on a man's birthday cake perhaps with a paste butterfly, ladybird or dragonfly on one of the leaves.

To make the blackberry, make a cone of blackish-violet paste. Place this on to a hooked 26-gauge wire; roll lots of tiny balls of paste and stick these all over the surface of the cone until it is completely covered. Roll out some green paste and cut a calyx; slide this up the wire and stick to the base. For the under-ripe blackberries, make in the same way but in mid-green paste.

The leaves are made the same way as the rose and ivy leaves featured in the previous lesson, but vein using a metal veiner for a strong veining effect. Make the flower in the same way as the buttercup using a small rose cutter with a cluster of yellow stamens in the centre of the flower.

## Finishing

Dust the under-ripe blackberries dark green one side and red the other. Varnish. The flower is dusted with a little green in the centre, while the leaves are dusted with a touch of copper-coloured petal dust, these too are varnished.

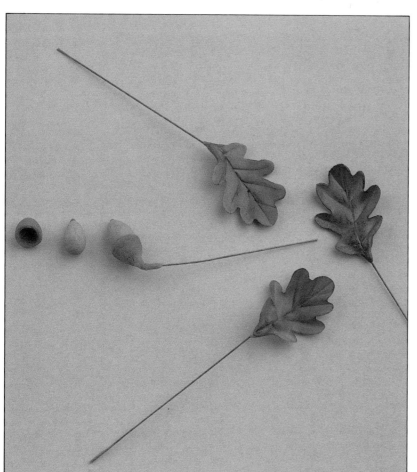

# Acorn

Acorns can be used on a man's cake or on a box of chocolates as a change from flowers; they can also be used with autumn flowers to make an unusual spray.

For the cup of the acorn, make a cone in mid-brown and mark with the end of a No. 2 tube to get a scalloped effect on the cup. The acorn is made by making a cone in green with a tiny tip of brown placed on the top. Stick into the cup using egg white. To make a wire acorn, mount a cone onto a wire and hollow out the cup, the wire should be at right angles to the cup; place the acorn in as before. The leaves are made as instructed on page 196.

Paint the acorn with green colouring mixed with clear spirit to give a natural effect to the acorn. Paint the leaves in a mixture of green and autumnal colours. Wire into a spray.

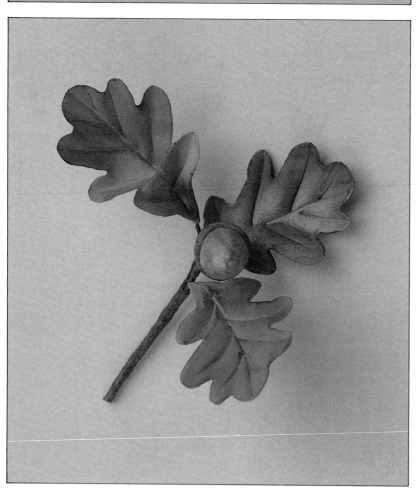

# Bess Rose

The Bess Rose is a small wild rose. It is a very dainty variety ideal for use on wedding, birthday and celebration cakes; it can also be adapted to make a Christmas Rose, green dust should then be brushed into the centre instead of using pale pink dust all over.

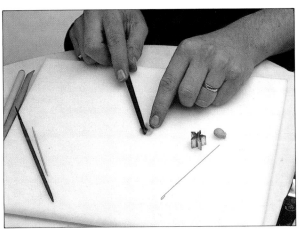

**1.** Make a Mexican hat and roll out the base using a paintbrush. Place the small calyx cutter over the top of the node and cut the calyx.

**2.** Make a hook on a piece of 26-gauge wire. Dip the hook in egg-white and thread through the calyx, pull through so that it embeds itself into the calyx.

**3.** Make a small ball of paste, place this on top of the hole made when the wire was inserted to act as a plug. Make a hole in the centre of the plug for stamens.

**4.** Roll out some white paste and cut out a five petal blossom. Place on a sponge and cup each petal slightly using a dog bone tool.

**5.** Brush some egg white on the calyx and turn the petal over; stick the calyx as shown onto the back of the rose.

**6.** Cup each petal onto a piece of foam to give it a cupped shape to the flower. Place some yellow stamens into the centre hole

# Forget-me-knots

Forget-me-knots with their cheery blue and yellow faces are useful in sprays based on a blue colour scheme.

**1.** Make some buds by putting some little, elongated blue rounds on pieces of 30-gauge wire and shape into a tiny cone. Cut out small-sized blossom using an ejector cutter.

**2.** Thread the blossom onto a piece of 30-gauge green wire which has been bent into a hook at one end.

**3.** Roll out a little yellow paste and cut a miniature yellow blossom shape, insert into the centre of the blue forget-me-knot using tweezers and a little egg white. Make a tiny hole in the centre using a cocktail stick.

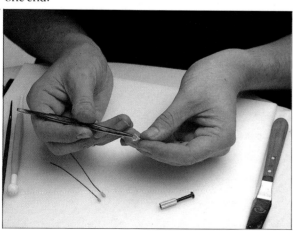

**4.** Take a white stamen in a pair of tweezers. Place the stamen into the centre of the flower.

**Finishing**
Wire into a spray as shown. You will need five to seven buds and three to five flowers per spray.

222

# Buttercups

Buttercups with their bright, yellow flowers give warmth to a spray and mix well with most other wild flowers.

**1.** Mould a cone of green paste. Place onto a piece of 28-gauge green wire which has already been hooked. Make a cavity using a ball tool as shown.

**2.** Remove the ball tool to leave a hollowed out cavity.

**3.** Roll out some green paste and cut a small calyx. Lift up on the modelling tool.

**4.** The finished calyx with its top piece in position, stick this with egg white.

**5.** Roll out some dark, yellow paste and cut out five petals using an apple blossom cutter.

**6.** Vein each petal and frill the edges gently with a cocktail stick.

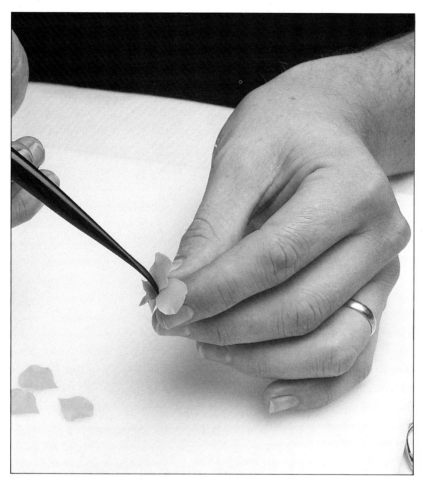

**7.** Using a little egg white, stick the petals into the centre of the prepared calyx overlapping each one in turn.

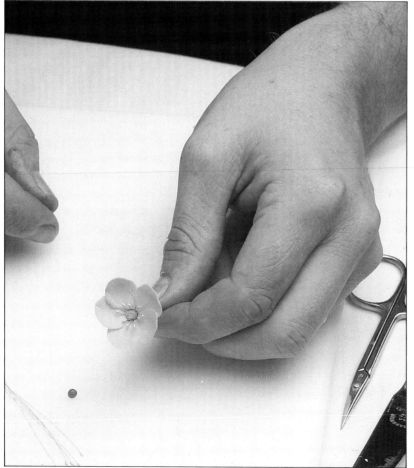

**Finishing**
To finish the buttercup place a ring of fine yellow stamens around the centre, then, taking a small ball of green paste roll in yellow semolina and stick into the centre. When dry, dust with a mixture of dark yellow petal dust and gold lustre to give a golden sheen to the petals.

# Making Flowers from Fresh Samples

# Using Fresh Flower Samples

Sugar flowers may be made from fresh specimens by using a wide variety of techniques.

To begin with, it is important to use simply constructed flowers. Pick fresh flowers from the garden after the dew has been dried by the morning sun or, if buying from the florist, check on seasonal availability as some varieties may need ordering in advance. Many florists will give you the odd head or leaf as it often seems unnecessary to buy a whole bunch of flowers when you only want one sample.

An assortment of orchid formers that can be made from empty drink tins cutting out the desired shape using floristry scissors. The ones shown are, at the back, an unwired Cymbidium orchid, front left, the Phalonopis (moth) orchid and the front right, the Dendrobium.

## Dendrobium Orchid

This orchid, also known as the Singapore orchid, comes in the off-white as shown and shades of pink and mauve. It is one of the many flowers for which there is no cutter available, but it is possible to reproduce this and many other flowers without cutters.

**1.** A spray of fresh Dendrobium orchids. Pick off a suitable flower to use as a model for the paste flower.

**2.** Using a modelling knife carefully disect the flower, you will notice that the Dendrobium has seven sections. Start working with the column, this is the small piece that comes into the throat; mould one in paste using your fresh one as a guide. To make the throat, roll out some paste and, using the fresh throat petal as a template, place onto the paste and cut round with a modelling knife. Remove the petal and support on foam to achieve the same soft shape as the fresh petal. Alternatively, lay on top of the fresh throat to set.

The two sepals or wing petals are cut from rolled sugarpaste again using the fresh petals as templates, veining the centre of each.

The main part is the back three sepals which are made in one piece. Cut out the shape from an empty drink tin and bend in the same shape as the fresh part. Roll out the paste and cut this piece again using the fresh petal as a template, then place on a former to dry.

**3.** This final picture shows the fresh and sugar orchids together, the sugar one is on the right. It has been assembled when dry using softened flower paste as a glue. When set, the orchid is dusted with a yellowish green petal dust.

227

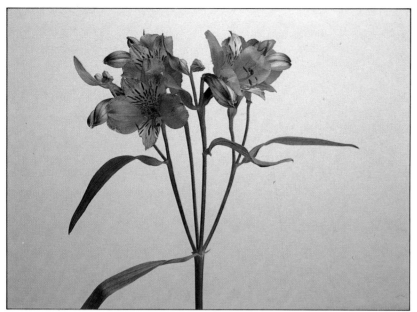

# Alstromeria

Alstromeria or Peruvian lily comes in many colours including red, yellow and cream as well as the pink shown. It is made using the individually wired petal principle used for orchids and foliage in Lesson 16.

**1.** Here the fresh spray of alstromeria with its delicate centre detail. Pick off a suitable flower as a sample.

**2.** As with the Dendrobium orchid, the fresh petals are used as templates. Take some pink paste, roll into a ball then squash, roll out using a paintbrush, retaining a thicker area towards the centre at one end. Place the petal on the paste so that the base covers the thicker part and, using a modelling knife, cut round the petal. Vein using the back of the real petal as the veiner and then place the piece of hooked 30-gauge wire into the thicker part. Place on sponge and mark the two curved veins and then turn over so the veins are on the back but in relief on the front of the petal. You need three large petals in pink and three of the smaller ones in off-white.

To make the stamen centre, squash grey paste onto six pink stamens and tape a piece of pink stamen cotton on to the end of a piece of wire, cutting in half lengthways to get a feathery top. Tape the grey tipped stamen onto the wire as shown. Dry along with the petals.

**3.** Dust and paint the flower taking the colours and the detail from the fresh petals to get the colouring correct. To assemble, take the centre stamen piece and place the three smaller petals in a triangular arrangement, then arrange the three outer petals in the gaps taping tightly to make sure they stay in position.

# Rubrem Lily

This large fragrant lily with its dark dense colouring looks attractive on a wedding cake and creates a very dramatic effect.

**1.** This picture shows the spray of fresh lilies. Pick a bloom and cut off the petals carefully with a modelling knife.

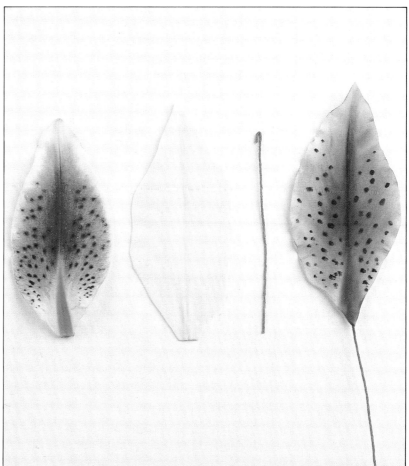

**2.** To make the lily petal, take the fresh petal left and use as template. Dust and paint as fresh sample.

# Scabious

This attractive summer garden flower comes in shades of blue and mauve making it an easy colour to use with pink, creams and lemons.

**1.** The fresh Scabious head with its soft frilly petals.

**2.** Remove a fresh petal and uncrumple it, lay on a piece of thin card and draw round it, then cut out to make a card template. Roll out some white paste, cut the petal shape. Using a modelling knife, cut the edge with tiny slits like those made for a spray carnation, then frill the edge, as shown. Dust in a blue or mauve shade straight away. After pleating the petal, as shown, place onto a cut out green daisy shape. Support with foam rubber sticking with egg white in the centre, continue all the way around, then make thin strips of white rolled paste, frill one end and then ruche up like french pleats. These sit inside the main petals. The stamens used were green matt-headed ones with tiny pieces of blue cotton placed in between them.

**3.** The sugar and real flower, side-by-side. The sugar flower is dusted blue and the fresh one shows one of the many shades of the Scabious.

# Fresh Flowers

**F**resh flowers were commonly used before sugar flowers became popular. Most royal iced wedding cakes would have a bride and groom or a silver vase filled with fresh flowers as a top feature decoration and these are still frequently requested.

**1.** Choose a fresh spray of carnations with nice strong stems and a good shape.

**2.** Cut off the head about 2.5cm (1in) down the stem behind the back of the flower ; if using buds or slightly open flowers, cut as for full blooms.

**3.** Taking a piece of anealed floristry wire, pierce the back of the calyx by pushing through the wire.

**4.** Bend the wire over to double up. Be careful to support the stem to stop the wire breaking the back of the calyx.

**5.** Taking a piece of 1cm (½in) wide floristry tape, tape down the wire starting on the calyx.

**6.** The finished wired spray carnation with a flexible wire stem.

# Ivy Leaf

**T**he principle shown here for wiring an ivy leaf may be applied to any type of foliage.

**1.** A sprig of ivy is cut off the leaves, leave a little piece of the stem at the base of the leaf.

**2.** Take a piece of fine rose wire and thread through the leaf as if using a needle and cotton.

**3.** Wrap the smaller piece of wire around the stem and the first piece of wire.

**4.** Using a piece of 1cm (½in) wide floristry tape, tape down the wire to finish off the leaf.

## Freesia

Cut off the separate freesia blooms with a pair of floristry scissors. Thread a piece of medium-gauge wire through the flower, bend the two pieces down and twist the smaller piece around the longer one. Tape down the flower and wire starting where the first wire was inserted.

# Fresh Flower Bouquets, Sprays and Posies

**1.** This posy is suitable for a large cake or as a spray for a bridesmaid. Wire into a posy in the same principle as the wired sugar posy in page 236. The posy is finished with a hand-made crochet posy frill and flowers include Doris pink, mauve and white freesias, Nigella (Love in a Mist), asparagus fern and gypsophila. The tails are made in white and lilac 3mm (⅛in) wide ribbon.

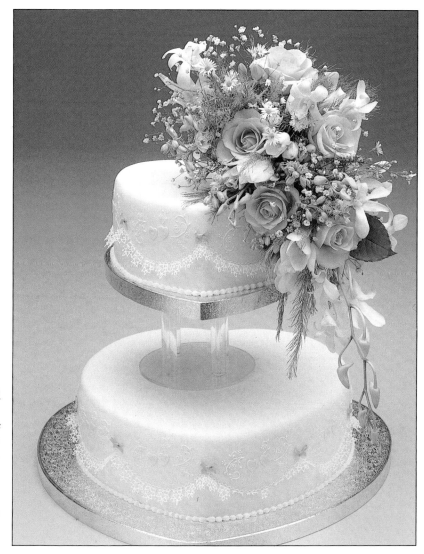

**2.** The two tier wedding cake shown here has a medium-sized bridal bouquet as a feature decoration. If a wedding is being done on a budget, a specially designed bride's bouquet could be put into the posy pick on the cake as the main decoration as she arrives at the reception. The bouquet features pale peach roses, white freesia, Dendrobium (Singapore) orchids, gypsophila, asparagus fern and miniature daisies.

# Silk and Fabric Flowers

Fabric flowers have many uses in cake decorating. Attractive and dramatic effects can be obtained using them on celebration and wedding cakes. Department stores, florists and cake decorating shops all stock an enormous array from tiny blossoms to large lilies and orchids, but only some of these are of a suitable size and shape for cake decorating.

The most realistic, but the most expensive, are the silk flowers, although many of the man-made fabric polyester type are now made to a high standard. Fabric flowers are also useful to use to perfect an arrangement that is to be made in sugarflowers as these are fragile to work with. Most fabric and silk flowers come on thick wire stems that have to be replaced with thinner 26 to 30-gauge wire which is wrapped round a piece of existing stem to make them more flexible. You can even colour fabric flowers; use white flowers from which delicate shades can be achieved with a firm-haired paintbrush and petal dust. Silk and fabric flowers can also be used on wedding cakes instead of sugar flowers particularly when time or money is short.

## Silver Vase

This picture shows fabric flowers arranged into vases. The smaller is in fact a silver cake pillar that has been upturned and filled with dry floristry foam or sugarpaste. The flowers used in the arrangement are lemon and white carnations, blossoms, gypsophila and foliage.

The larger silver vase is filled with an arrangement of pink and white fuchsias, carnations and foliage.

## Bridal Bouquet

**1.** This large bridal bouquet is arranged in the same way as the green and peach orchid and rose in Lesson 16. reproduced on a larger scale and placed into a posy pick on a wedding cake offering an alternative to sugar flowers.

234

# Flower Sprays and Corsages

# Sprays & Posies

**T**he Victorian posy always has a rose as a central focal point with rings of flowers and foliage working out, or a more natural arrangement with five small leg sprays tapered out, with the cavities filled with ribbons and more pulled blossoms.

The flowers and foliage needed to produce the following posy and straight spray are: three spray carnations, sixteen five petal basic pulled blossoms, nine buds and five medium ivy leaves.

**1.** Using floristry tape cut in half, start by taping three blossoms together all on the level.

**2.** Then make one pink and one green double ribbon loop from 3mm (⅛in) ribbon and position either side of the blossoms. Place a bud in between each ribbon. Note how the posy is being worked in triangles at this stage.

**3.** Now place another blossom behind each bud, shaping into a slight curve. It is important not to place the flowers too low. If you do, you will end up with a cone shape. The curve on a basin bottom is approximately the angle you should be working towards. Note the dominant triangle shape.

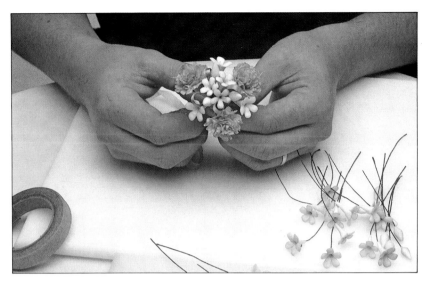

**4.** Take the spray carnations and place one in each of the gaps between the blossoms; tape tightly. Make two pink and two green medium-sized double figure-of-eight loops and position alternately green and pink around the edge. The shape now changes from a triangle formation to a circular.

**5.** Place the remaining blossoms and buds at random around the posy where needed.

**6.** To finish the basic assembly, tape the five ivy leaves spaced at regular intervals around the posy. In between two of the leaves, tape two loops with double tails. These are single figure-of-eight loops, but with extra long tails. The tails are the front of the posy.

**7.** Insert wires and tape through posy holder.

**8.** Wrap the floristry tape around the back, tape around several times to stop the posy holder slipping down the wire. Tape firmly to secure.

**9.** Continue taping right off the edge of the wires, then cut off the excess tape leaving the overlap on the end of the wires.

**10.** Fold the excess flap over to cover all the ends so as not to leave sharp wires exposed, then tape back up the handle until you run out of tape.

**11.** The finished posy.

**12.** Here is the same posy shown in a tiny floristry posy holder, it has been carefully cut around the edge to produce an attractive scallop.

# Inverted V Sprays

The flowers shown are those needed for both the inverted V and reverse S curve sprays. They consist of five spray carnations, seven ivy leaves, twelve buds and about twenty-eight blossoms.

**1.** Begin by making the two legs of the spray which are both identical. First of all position a pink swallow bow and then two buds followed by five blossoms and a double green loop.

**2.** Continue with buds and flowers and place a carnation centrally, finish with pink double figure-of-eight bow. Repeat to make the second leg.

**3.** Make a posy as previously described using the remaining flowers, a double bow and three figure-of-eight loops.

**4.** The four ivy leaves are positioned together at the top and the remaining ivy leaf at the base of the posy leaving a gap either side for the legs.

**5.** Tape the first leg into the posy, taping tightly so it does not move.

**6.** Tape in the third leg and bind all wires firmly together. The finished inverted V spray would be placed in a posy spray pick, if being used on a cake.

# Corsage

Corsages nowadays are used mainly as a decoration on garments for weddings, but several years ago they were given by gentlemen when taking a lady out to dinner. Sugar flower corsages are suitable for small cakes or knife sprays or they may be given as a gift.

**1.** Make all the pieces from the directions given on Page 203. Start off by taping the back cupped sepal to the throat as shown.

**2.** The two small sepals sit with their curved sides upwards either side of the cupped back sepal. Place the two larger curved petals at the bottom of the flower as shown. Make a small sausage in yellow paste and stick into the throat and vein in half.

**3.** Dust some yellow petal dust into the centre of the throat. Mix a little plum petal dust with some clear spirit and paint some fine feathery lines around the frilled part as shown. Finish off the painting with some spots on the throat.

**4.** Using a soft pink petal dust, brush around the throat and at the base of the sepals.

**5.** Take one Cymbidium orchid, one piece of gypsophila, two leaves, a yellow bow, plus a tulle bow.

**6.** Tape together as shown.

# Spray Carnation Corsage

**1.** You will need two carnations, one bud, two ivy leaves, one piece of sword fern and a double figure-of-eight bow.

**2.** Start off with the sword fern, then the carnations and continue with the other pieces.

**3.** The final stage is the positioning of the ribbon bow. This can be in a contrast colour, as shown, or the same shade as the flowers.

## Blackberry Box

A spray of blackberries makes an alternative to a spray of flowers on a chocolate box. This is ideal for a Father's day or Mum's birthday gift. It would also be suitable for a husband and wife as a joint gift.

## Gift Box

A lovely idea is to make a small spray of flowers to be attached to a small cake box used when people are unable to attend a wedding or celebration. It has been tied with a 3mm (⅛in) powder blue ribbon and then has a small spray of Bess rose, forget-me-nots and ivy leaves. The silver writing adds the finishing touch to the box.

## Knife Spray

When decorating a wedding cake, it is a lovely touch to make a knife spray to match. Make a small straight spray in flowers to match those used on the cake. Take a piece of 30-gauge covered wire and thread through the spray twisting at the back of the spray. Bring the wires around the side of the knife where the blade meets the handle, bring to the centre back and twist the wires together tightly. Cut off excess wire and fold back towards the spray.

# Bridal Bouquet

This large spray, based on a small bridal bouquet, is wired in the same way in fresh or silk flowers. This size spray is suitable as shown for two or three tier wedding cakes and can be made up to two or three times this size if required. There is a lot of initial preparation as you will need several hours to make the flowers. This spray contains Cymbidium orchids, roses, pulled blossoms, ivy and various foliage and gypsophilas but other flowers could be used, if desired. Usually this type of spray does not include ribbons.

**1.** Make the flowers shown. The main ones being five Cymbidium orchids, four roses, two rose buds. You will need several sprays of gypsophilas, two to three dozen pulled blossoms and an assortment of variegated ivy and other foliage.

**2.** Start off with a small ivy leaf, then add the first buds. The two rose buds are progressively opening up as you work along the spray.

**3.** Place the first orchid in position. You will have to tape this firmly. Make sure the taping is really tight as large flowers need supporting.

**4.** Then place another rose and orchid. Note the zig zag effect going from one side to the other. Leave aside at this stage and go on to the separate posy.

**5.** Now you need to wire a separate posy for the top. Start off as shown with the remaining two roses and another orchid.

**6.** Finish off by using the last orchid and all of the remaining flowers and foliage.

**7.** Tape the posy to the first part of the spray, make sure to tape these firmly together using full width floristry tape.

**8.** The finished bouquet.

**9.** This type of spray and most of the others show should be put into a posy or spray pick. This is a white food-grade plastic vial; the one shown comes with a little base so that once the base is cut the spray can be removed and the vial placed back into its stand to hold the spray. Stick the pick into position on the cake. This spray is placed at an angle but be careful not to place too near the edge of the cake or the flowers will look unbalanced, spoil the effect, and may crack the paste.

**10.** Continue pushing the vial in until it is level with the top of the cake surface. Fill the cavity with sugarpaste to hold the wires in place. On no account must the wires go straight into the cake. For a small spray, the top from a fibre tip pen can be used in place of a posy pick.

**11.** The top tier of the wedding cake with the bouquet in position. Because a larger spray will trail below the board it is best to take the bouquet to the reception separately and then insert into the pick once the cake is set up. If this is not possible, you will have to bend the spray then, once in position, it will have to be carefully pushed back into shape.

# Wired Sprays

**H**aving mastered the art of flower-making, it is time to go on to combine them in the form of sprays and arrangements.

There are a great variety of wired sprays and corsages in many different styles to choose from. Those covered in this chapter include the basic types that are suitable to use on celebration and wedding cakes. The principle is not unlike that used by a florist when producing bridal bouquets, posies and corsages for a wedding in fresh flowers. The only difference is that fresh flowers are easier to arrange because you can undo the spray if not happy with it, but sugar flowers do not like that sort of treatment as the petals and calyxes get broken. Generally sugar flowers have to be treated with loving care, and should not be packed too densely or they crack and break. Once the cake is covered or even before it is baked, it is best to have a visual idea of what type of spray you are going to put on the cake. The most important elements are colour, shape and proportion.

### Colour
When flowers are put together the overall colour scheme tends to become more intense. When using dark colours, try to make the smaller flowers in the dark colours rather than the large focal flowers as this would make the overall effect too dense. Generally a florist would use not more than two or at the most, three main colours so bear this in mind too. A flower arrangement nearly always includes some foliage as a finishing touch and this is equally true for sugar sprays. Ribbons may be an important addition and again can dramatically change the finished effect. Choose neutral coloured ribbons as these blend best with the flowers. If using several colours together always place them together off the cake and see if they tone in with each other before arranging.

### Shape
The shape of a spray of flowers can dramatically change the overall appearance of the cake, but with practice you will be able to look at a cake and assess the best type of spray to use.

### Proportion
The proportion of the flowers is a very important point to consider. There is nothing worse than a spray with all the flowers out of proportion and when combining several different flower types, it can take some time to work out. The easiest solution is to make the sugar flowers the same size as the fresh ones, alternatively, make all of them to half scale. Pulled and finger flowers are useful as you make these to whatever size you require, while you can be a little restricted when using cutters as there may not always be a cutter of a suitable size available.

If you are new to wired flower arranging, start off with fabric flowers as you can bend these and squash them without breaking them. Once the basic shape has been mastered you can then duplicate it using sugar flowers. Most silk and polyester flowers are on thick wires unsuitable for small sprays so you will need to cut the wire off leaving about 1.5cm (⅝in), then tape a piece of 26-gauge wire to this and bind with floristry tape. Fabric flowers can be repeatedly used in the same or different sprays.

Once you have made your chosen flowers, dust to the required shade and bind with floristry tape. The Nile green colour is suitable for most sprays, but dark green and white are also used from time to time. Depending on the size of the spray and flowers, cut the tape in half or quarters lengthwise. If you have made a mass of flowers and have two or three sprays to make for a wedding cake, split the flowers up before beginning the first spray so that all the sprays will be equal and you will not run out of flowers.

If new to sugar flower arranging, it is advisable to work on a sheet of foam then you can lay the spray down in between stages or if you drop anything it will not break. When taping, tape firmly, if not the flowers will move about and you will have problems creating and maintaining a shape.

### Ribbons
Ribbon loops play an important part in making posies and sprays. For further information on making loops and tails, see lesson on Ribbons in Book 1.

# Competitions and Commissions

# Cake Commissions

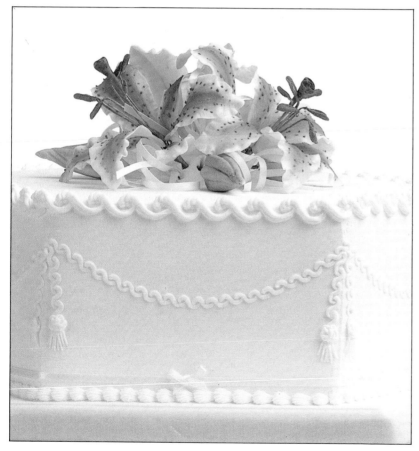

## Portions from a Cake

If the cake is commissioned you will have to find out the number for the wedding breakfast, the evening reception and any additional pieces for people unable to attend or to be sent away. Once you have these numbers add them together to give you a number to calculate the size on.

For further information on portions from a cake, see lesson on Designing a Cake in Book One of this series.

## Pricing Cakes

How much do I charge? This question causes so many problems and it is always a difficult one to answer because many factors have to be taken into account when pricing a cake.

There are two main types of cake produced: the commercial cake – this would be the type of cake your local baker produces. He usually works out his expenses on the ingredients for the cake itself, then adds the labour costs and his mark up. This is fairly easy to do as he has all his invoices in front of him, he knows how much everything costs, how much he pays his staff and what his profit margin should be.

Secondly, there is the home commissioned cake – this includes icing a cake for a commission, friend or family. A commercial cake should be easy to produce and not terribly labour intensive. Most people at home spend a lot longer icing a cake, often doing a little at a time rather than completing the cake in a day from start to finish. Pricing becomes even more difficult when friends or family are involved. Often the cake is given as a gift but when you work out the cost of the ingredients alone you will find you are being more than generous. Listed below are some different ways of structuring your prices.

Work out the total cost of all the ingredients and add two or three times that amount depending on the

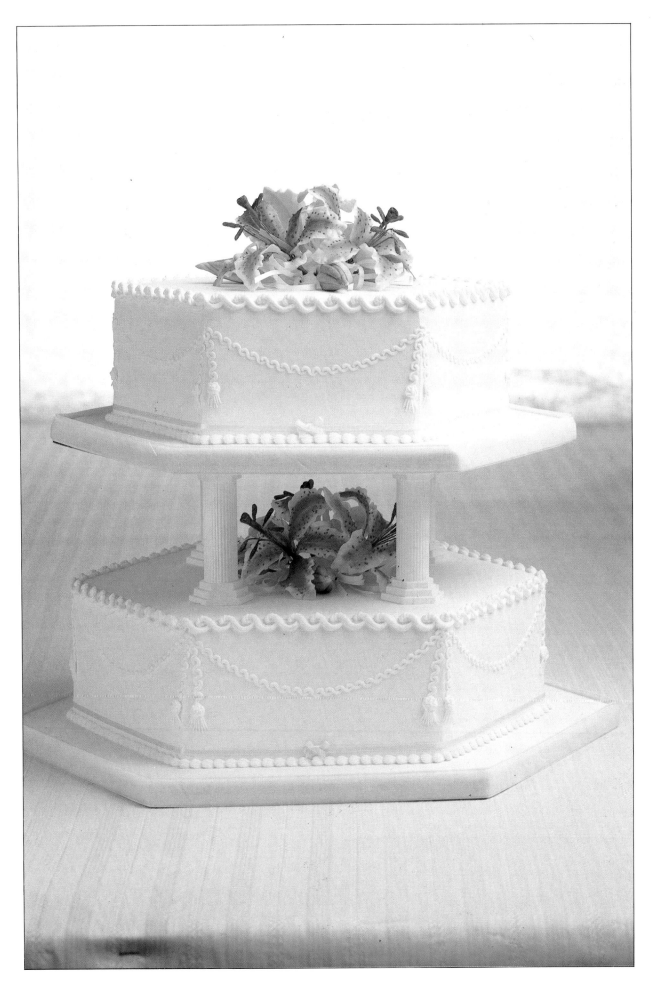

complexity of the design and the hours spent working on the cake. The price can be worked out per kilo or pound for the basic cake coated and decorated and then charge extra per spray of flowers or for special features. Alternatively, the costing may be made on all the ingredients, then work out an hourly rate for labour, remember shopping, washing-up and clearing-up time, all these things add up and should be taken into consideration.

Do not under-estimate yourself. Many people feel that they cannot charge a reasonable fee because they are not professional. Today that does not mean much, professional is only a term for someone who has been to college and works in industry full or part-time.

Many people work from home and produce work of a very high standard. When you give a quotation for the price of a cake, cover yourself by saying it is only approximate. We all learn from our mistakes and often someone chooses a design from a book which you think is going to take about an hour and it ends up taking a whole evening to do and you must be sure that you do not lose out. If a customer is making their own cake it can sometimes take two to three hours to level it off and to fill-in large holes and cracks. All these things will affect the final price.

It is nice to offer the hire of a knife and stand. Although it is an initial outlay, by charging a hire fee you will soon be able to recover your costs and

then be able to buy some new shapes maybe a perspex, spiral or S-stand. Make sure you have your stand and knife insured, and that your name is clearly marked on the base. Often they are put into the kitchen at the end of a reception and it is easy for them to get lost in a busy hotel kitchen.

# Commission Form

When taking details for a cake commission it is advisable to have a standard form prepared so that you are sure to get all the details from the client. Use the following example as a guide.

| Wedding Cake Order Form | | |
|---|---|---|
| Name of customer: | Shape of cake: | Number of tiers:          Sizes: |
| Address: | Cutting cake          yes/no | |
| | Base colour: | |
| Telephone: | Secondary colour: | Other themes in wedding (eg. bows, birds, butterflies etc.) |
| Date of wedding: | | |
| Viewing date: | Board type: | |
| Design roughs submitted by: | Swatches of bridal material provided          yes/no | |
| **Costings** Finished cake: | Flowers (type and colour): | Special instructions (eg. inscriptions, runouts, lacework etc.) |
| Stand and knife: | Florist's name: | |
| Delivery charge: | Address: | Knife spray          yes/no |
| Deposit paid: | | Stand and knife hire          yes/no |
| Balance due on approval at viewing: | Telephone: | |

# Competition Cake

Entering competitions is a very challenging, yet most satisfying aspect of cake decoration and sugarcraft. Many hours can be spent on any one part of a cake, whether it be the coating, linework, figure-work or the lettering. To give yourself a good chance of winning, total dedication to your work is required. This can be very demanding on your time, so do ensure you are able to allocate sufficient to do justice to your exhibit. It could be many weeks before you see any reasonable work worth entering, but persevere and hopefully you will achieve your aim.

### Understanding the Schedule
First of all check that you are eligible to enter the class you wish to exhibit in. It may be a novice or open class, or it may be that you need to be a member of a particular body or organisation. It is important to read the specification very carefully and to be aware of what the class is requesting in terms of size, cost, presentation, and the accepted use of edible or non-edible decorations. Note also whether you need to use a real cake or if cake dummies are allowed in the particular class you wish to enter.

Remember to complete and return the entry form with the entry fee if required. Check the date of the competition and the time of delivery for your exhibit; give yourself extra time on the actual day in case of delays or breakages.

### Designing the Cake
Try to be as original as possible with your cake design, do something to attract the eye of the judges. Numerous ideas can be gleaned from greeting cards and gift wrapping paper, not only for the motif, figure or animal, but also for ideas on lettering styles and inscriptions. If you intend to use any templates for off-pieces, for example runout collars, it is better to measure your cake after the final coat and then design your collar to fit exactly. Otherwise, work to accurate

dimensions and templates throughout the production of the cake.

### Materials
Use good quality ingredients to give you a good quality exhibit. In the case of royal icing use a fine bridal icing (confectioner's) sugar. Strain the egg white or reconstituted albumen before mixing to remove any fine lumps or impurities which could affect coating. Sugarpaste cakes need a good coating to win points, so use the paste recipe or product which you know works best for you. Keep a record of colours used for your various materials in case you need to re-match. Royal icing can be weighed and a set number of drops of colour added, make a note of the ratio and use it again if necessary. Sugarpaste can also be colour matched by mixing a strong shade of the eventual tint you require, a portion of this mixture can then be weighed and mixed into a decided weight of white paste. For example 30g (1oz) of coloured paste to 1kg (2lbs) of white sugarpaste.

### Cake Dummies
Use the highest quality cake dummies you can afford. A smooth unblemished surface to start with will make coating and covering much easier. If you have to use a real cake for your exhibit, do ensure that you achieve a good smooth coating of marzipan on which to work with your icing or sugarpaste. Coat the cake dummy and board separately to create a good finish on both. The two can be brought together when assembly of all the various parts of the cake commences.

## Hints and Tips

For royal icing coating, add a few drops of cold water to the icing for each coat. This will soften the icing and help achieve a smoother finish. The final coat should be very thin, working with considerable pressure on the side scraper and straight edge for the top surface.

Smooth down the surface of your coatings with a sharp knife or sandpaper – except on the final coat, when scratches would be visible. Try to cover the take-off mark on the side of your royal iced cake with a linework panel or other parts of the side decoration.

Use fine tubes when outlining runout pieces or collars to give a degree of delicacy to your work.

Ensure a good sheen on runout work by placing the units near a gentle heat immediately after flooding. Use an anglepoise lamp.

Linework is an important part of the finish of your cake and can mean a considerable amount of points towards your final result. Use No1 and No0 tubes along with some work done in No00. For curved lines a slightly softer consistency of icing will create a better flow. Ensure good joins are made on linework and pipe an equal distance from the adjacent line. As a rule for piping, the distance between lines should be similar to the thickness of the tube you are using at that particular time.

### Packing and Exhibiting
Once your cake is completed, attach your staging tickets to the cake board with a little glue, do this neatly and keep the labels straight and clean. Place the cake carefully into a good strong cake box with a secure lid. Many serious exhibitors have wooden carrying boxes made with a foam covered sliding base section to make positioning in the box easier, these carrying boxes should also have a strong handle with which to carry them.

Label your exhibit box, especially if you have more than one, making staging easier on arrival at the competition venue.

Well before leaving for the venue, check that you have the schedule for reference, and your admission tickets.

On arrival at the venue, don't remove the cake from the box until you have found out exactly where to place your exhibit. Then stage your cake in its allocated space, being careful not to damage other exhibits that may already be on the table. Place the cake in the correct viewing position, so that the judges first look is the one you want them to see.

After the judging, whether or not you are a winner, try to find the judges of your cake and discuss your exhibit with them. Most of them will be quite co-operative in this way. By talking to the judges you can make notes about aspects of your cakes that could be improved, or altered. Do not be discouraged by the fact you do not win anything for your first entry, or even subsequent entries. Keep trying, use your experiences and put the judges comments to good use to improve your skills, knowledge and ability.

# The Wedge Cake

The wedge cake was popular at one time and you may get an occasional request to do a cake with a wedge. This is when a wedge of the cake is cut out then tied with ribbon and replaced. The wedge must be taken into consideration when designing the cake, for example, a continuous run-out collar could not be used. It is best to decide on the basic design before cutting the wedge as most designs are worked out upon six, eight or twelve repeating segments and the wedge would represent one whole section. Work out a pattern so you know the size

of the portion to be cut. Find the centre of the cake after two coats of icing using a compass or a circle of paper folded into quarters, and then mark the edge of the cake in the two places it is to be cut. Using a sharp knife and a rule, mark a line from the centre dot to each of the outer lines then hold the ruler vertically up the side and mark the two down lines.

## Cutting through the sugar and cake
It is very important to use a saw bladed knife to cut the wedge. Use an even sawing action to cut through the icing on the top then move onto the side and repeat the sawing action holding the knife vertically against the cake. Once the icing has been sawn through use a fine bladed sharp knife and cut through the marzipan and the cake using a gentle sawing action making sure that the knife is straight. Take care not to cut into the cake board. Remove any crumbs and give the cake a final coating of icing. Once this final coat is dry you only need to saw through the icing to release the wedge.

## Tying with ribbon
Take a piece of satin ribbon 3-5cm (1½-2in) and 70-100cm (24-36in) long. This can either be in white or in a shade to match or contrast with the coating of the cake. In order to prevent the ribbon being stained by the cake it should be sandwiched in between a

folded strip of greaseproof (waxed) paper. The paper should reach up to the start of the marzipan and be long enough to wrap round both sides of the wedge. Once replaced into the cake only the front of the ribbon should be showing and the paper should not be visible. Place the wedge back into the cake and tie the ribbon in a bow with trailing tails, trim the end of the tails to equal lengths and cut into an inverted V-shape. With the wedge in position the cake can be decorated. Use paper clips to clip the rolled up tails onto the ribbon so they do not get in your way when decorating the cake. The bride and groom can then simply release the piping and remove the customary wedge. Some competitions, especially when a percentage of points are given for the cake itself, will ask for a wedge cake. This makes it easier for the judges to remove the wedge for inspection and tasting. It will always state in the schedule if a wedge is required.

## Specialist Work
If you are entering modelling or flower work for a competition it is advisable to invest in a display case. Covering an exhibit helps protect it from being touched and consequently damaged, it also protects it from dust. A small dish of silica gel inside the case helps to keep the atmosphere around the exhibit moisture free.

# Competition Schedule

The following is an illustration of the type of schedule you might be asked to follow for a competition. The resulting cake is illustrated on page 249.

**Schedule Sugarpaste - Open Class**
A celebration cake of not more than 22cm (9in) diameter. On a suitable base not exceeding 30cm (12in). The overall depth of the finished exhibit must not exceed 10cm (4in). The cake to be coated with sugarpaste and decorative work may include royal icing, sugarpaste, pastillage or moulded flowers. These may be wired and have artificial stamens. Ribbons and tulle may be used.

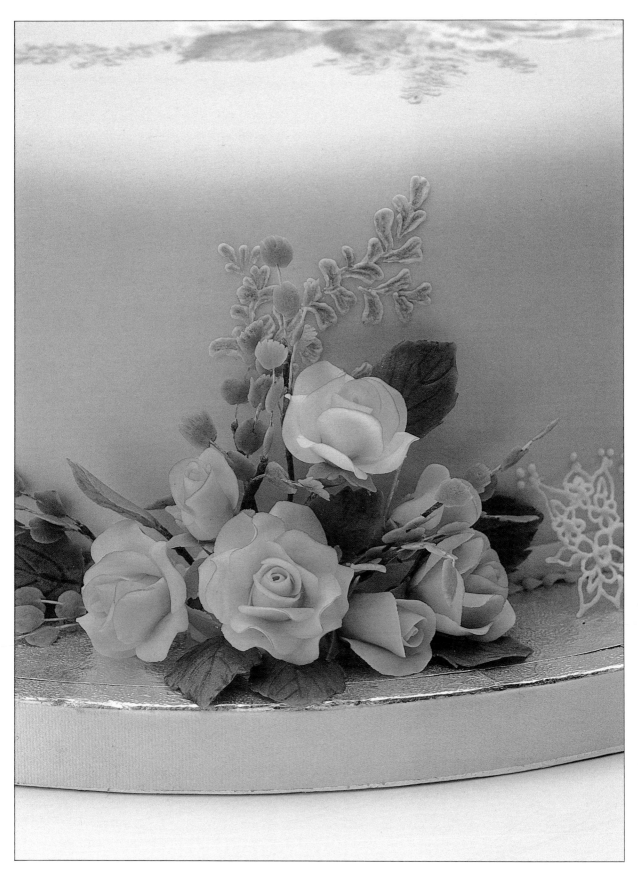

**Interpretation**

A Schedule like this placed very few restrictions on the competitor except for the dimensions. The board has to be carefully measured along with the cake. As the overall depth must not exceed 10cm (4in), including the board, a conventional floral spray on top would have made the exhibit too high and it would have been disqualified. The options were a very low arrangement of flowers or a completely flat decoration.

For her entry, Cynthia Venn opted for a design using brush embroidery, continuing the theme of roses down to the board with an arrangement of moulded roses, surrounded by lace pieces.